Georgia's Cakes

Georgia's Cakes

A step-by-step masterclass to make every cake a showstopper

Georgia Green

PAVILION

Meet Georgia

Believe it or not, I never dreamed of being a baker. I flitted between photography, art, fashion and animation before finally finding my feet in flour. I'm here to share with you my journey, my experience, but most importantly, my recipes, tips and tricks to arm you with the arsenal you need to create cakes that you thought only existed in Parisian patisseries.

From cook to book.

It wasn't until I discovered Le Cordon Bleu in London that I had even considered this to be my career path. During my last years of school, I was studying Maths, Photography and Art. With a mathematical brain and an artistic flair, architecture was the obvious direction to take (at least according to my careers advisor). To follow in my father's footsteps as an architect would also guarantee me a job and a 'successful future'… Problem? I had no interest or passion in buildings. I made the decision to decline my place at Nottingham University and took a year out of education. A couple of art courses and a travelling trip later, I attended an Art Foundation Course and was overwhelmed with what the art world had to offer. Graphics, design, technical drawing, fashion, fine art, textiles – you name it. Spoilt for choice, I ended up specializing in animation. The idea of drawing cartoons all day and having a job at Disney was what I had thought to be the ultimate dream at the time, but unfortunately, the good ol' days of pencil drawings and modelling plasticine have long gone. To be an animator in the millennial era entails endless hours of sitting at a computer desk working on complex digital animating programmes, which wasn't exactly what I was expecting, nor did I feel a connection to it.

Throughout this time, I had discovered my underlying love for food. Naturally, baking made the most sense to me because of all the numbers, weighing, timing, and of course, licking the bowl clean. I was using any excuse to cook and experiment and was even incorporating food elements into my animations during my studies. While animating a sneezing macaron and a laughing lemon sounds like fun, it got to a point where I was in constant search for something new to try, until I came across Le Cordon Bleu. From the moment I entered those doors in Bloomsbury Square in central London, I knew this was the world I wanted to be in.

Six months training in classical French patisserie and working in a bakery in central London gave me such an insight into the culinary world – both the cooking and the business side. Leaving home at 5.30am and delirious from not seeing daylight during the winter hours made me question this profession; however, seeing customers eat and enjoy the food that I had prepared with my own hands made it all worthwhile. That feeling was so precious that I craved it more. Over time, my reputation as a baker grew amongst my family and friends and bespoke cake orders became more regular, so much so that I decided to leave my job and continue on my own as Georgia's Cakes full-time.

I've always been a firm believer in 'everything happens for a reason', and though my path wasn't a clear straight road, it brought me to the perfect destination. I have been running my cake business, Georgia's Cakes, since the summer of 2015, I've held multiple cake decorating workshops in the UK and abroad, I've launched and maintained a YouTube channel with over 300,000 subscribers, I have grown an Instagram following of over 200,000, appeared on national television, and now own and run my own cake decorating studio, Baker Street TLV, with a fellow baker in Tel Aviv.

I thought it would only make sense and would be such a pleasure to share my knowledge, passion and, of course, my cake secrets with you. I hope you enjoy this book and, most importantly, learn a lot.

THE
ESSENTIALS

In order to make and decorate a beautiful cake, you have to be fully equipped and prepared before you start. Cake decorating requires specific equipment that you may not already own, certain ingredients that you may not be familiar with and, of course, the understanding of certain baking terms and how they differ from one another.

Equipment

Knowing your whisk from your palette knife.

Unsurprisingly, baking and cake decorating requires specific kitchen equipment. Some equipment is more generic, such as bowls and pans, whereas others may need to be specially purchased. Even though investing in certain equipment may sound intimidating, I can promise you that it will save you time, make the process easier and, therefore, more enjoyable overall.

Plus, it could even save you money in the long run. Most cake decorators who end up running their own business all start with the most basic equipment, usually labelled for 'beginners', mostly made of plastic and not very durable. Something that I learned very quickly is that the better the quality of equipment, the better the results. So, if you're serious about cake decorating, then get your checklist ready.

Kitchen equipment

BAKING TRAYS/OVEN TRAYS AND BAKING PAPER It's helpful to have several baking trays/oven trays to hand. I prefer using baking/oven trays that fit the full size of the oven, as it's more efficient using the space on the tray to the maximum capacity. Non-stick baking paper or parchment is ideal for lining baking/oven trays and cake tins to prevent the baked goods from sticking to the trays/tins.

BOWLS You will probably have these already, but various-sized bowls are helpful for all different purposes. Whether it's weighing ingredients, splitting cake batters, melting chocolate, or even storing items, I would recommend having access to heatproof bowls as well as regular mixing bowls.

BREAD KNIFE You will see later in this book that I rely on a bread knife to cut and torte my cakes.

NON-STICK HEATPROOF SILICONE MATS Not essential, but using a silicone mat helps to make some beautiful cake decorations as well as saving on baking paper for making some recipes (such as meringue kisses and meringue lollipops – see pages 138–41). It's important to make sure any silicone mats you use are heatproof and oven-safe, too!

PANS Many of my recipes require a saucepan, especially one that a stand mixer bowl can fit over/inside.

PARING KNIFE A smaller sharp knife comes in handy when making decorations and sharpening buttercream corners.

SCISSORS A good pair of scissors is a must! Use a pair of clean scissors that can cut through paper and plastic easily, and keep them separate from any office stationery so there's no cross-contamination.

SIEVE A regular sieve to sift flour, icing sugar or cocoa powder to remove any unwanted lumps.

WHISK I use a hand whisk to mix ingredients, and the whisk attachment on a stand mixer for incorporating air.

WIRE (COOLING) RACK A separate wire (cooling) rack is really useful for placing hot baked items on to allow good air circulation as they cool and also to avoid damaging the work surface underneath.

Cake decorating equipment

CAKE TINS To produce a beautiful-looking cake, it all starts with the sponge. Having the best possible cake tins will make all the difference: tall with straight sides and sharp, right-angled corners. Any sort of springform or loose-based tin won't achieve the same results.

DIGITAL SCALES Baking isn't like cooking. It's a science and therefore we need to be precise in what we do; hence, we weigh everything. All my recipes are weighed in grams, which is a universal measurement and guarantees consistent results every time (for this book, we also include equivalent UK imperial and US cup measurements alongside the metric measures). Digital scales are a must-have in the kitchen!

FLORIST TAPE When using flowers to decorate a cake, they must be prepared correctly using florist tape (this is explained later in the book). This tape is available from any florist shop or online – I prefer using dark green tape to blend into the flowers as much as possible.

FOOD/SUGAR THERMOMETER My buttercream recipe requires heating up egg whites and sugar to a specific temperature in order to make it safe to eat. A food/sugar thermometer is the only way to know if it has reached this temperature, and therefore is another essential.

HEATPROOF RUBBER SPATULA A rubber spatula allows you to clean each bowl of batter so there is zero waste. A heatproof spatula also gives the possibility of cooking ingredients at higher temperatures without it melting!

OVEN THERMOMETER If you're a serious baker, then I would advise using an oven thermometer. It's a small metal dial that sits inside your oven and reads the exact temperature inside. The reason why this piece of equipment is so important is that every oven is different, which can seriously affect your bakes without you even realizing. I once worked out of an oven which was actually around 15–20 degrees hotter than what I had programmed it to, so I had to set it at 150°C/130°C fan/gas 2 in order to get an accurate reading of 170°C/150°C fan/gas 3½.

PAINTBRUSHES You can probably get by without them, but food-safe paintbrushes can be used to add small delicate details to cakes and other treats. **Note:** 'food-safe' paintbrushes are made in a way that ensures bristles do not fall out onto food, unlike regular paintbrushes that are likely to do so.

PALETTE KNIFE A step-palette knife is a must. This is where the handle is higher than the blade of the knife and therefore doesn't get in the way when you're working with it. Personally, I prefer smaller palette knives as you have more control over them, however, it's down to personal preference as many sizes are available.

PIPING NOZZLES/TIPS I believe there is no limit to the amount of piping nozzles/tips one can own. I would always recommend having a few different-sized star nozzles/tips as well as plain round ones, too. More intricate piping nozzles/tips are used for specific cake designs and are usually much harder to use, but they are also fun to experiment with.

SIDE SCRAPER A tall metal scraper with sharp corners makes all the difference to your cake. Plastic scrapers don't provide the same clean finish that a metal one does and isn't as durable either.

STAND MIXER I admit, a stand mixer is quite an investment, but also a life-saver! There are certain recipes that can only be achieved by using a stand mixer and it will save you so much time in the long run.

TURNTABLE Your new best friend! In order to work at the cake from all angles, you need a turntable. The better quality the turntable, the smoother it will glide, which therefore results in higher quality cakes.

Disposables

CAKE BOARDS/CAKE DRUMS These boards are what we build and assemble our cakes on. Once cakes are filled and stacked they can get heavy, so make sure the cake boards are strong enough to hold the weight of a cake. Either double-thick cake boards or cake drums are best!

CAKE BOXES Transporting a cake is something I cover later in the book. The best way is to place the cake inside a cake box. There are many types of boxes available, some reusable for your own usage and also disposable if you're giving the cake away.

DOWELS These are wooden or plastic sticks that are used when stacking a tiered cake, which you will learn how to use later in the book.

PIPING BAGS I use a variety of small and large piping bags depending on what I'm making. I find reusable piping bags are hard to clean properly, so I would recommend using disposable piping bags.

STRAWS Regular drinking straws come into play when applying flowers to cake, but also when stacking cakes on top of each other as explained later on in the book. Plastic straws are the strongest and easiest option to use, but bamboo straws and wooden skewers (easily cut to height using scissors or a small, sharp knife) for stacking cakes are great alternatives. Paper straws tend to get soft over time but can be used to apply fresh flowers to a cake.

Ingredients

We live in a world where we're spoiled for choice with ingredients. There are new variations of spreadable butters, vegan spreads, gluten-free flours and longer-lasting creams. What we tend to forget is that baking is a science and, while we can experiment, it can't be messed with. Alternative ingredients can answer people's prayers; however, baking with them may not work out for the best. Understanding ingredients and their purposes will make you realize why certain methods are carried out and how alterations can affect the end result. Luckily, my recipes don't require too many ingredients, so as long as you have an understanding of the basics, you'll be able to bake stress-free!

Butter

When I say butter, I *mean* butter. Not oil, spreadable versions, or margarine. Just 100% butter. I personally get a little put off seeing how many hidden ingredients can sneak their way into a cake without you even realizing. Butter is a necessity to a cake's flavour, therefore avoid any additional ingredients that may affect it. The better tasting the butter, the better tasting the cake!

EXAMPLE MARGARINE INGREDIENTS
Vegetable oils 65% (containing 52% canola and sunflower oil), water, salt, emulsifiers (soy lecithin, 471), preservative 202, food acid (lactic), milk solids, maltodextrin, natural colour (beta-carotene), vitamins A and D, flavour

UNSALTED BUTTER INGREDIENTS
Cow's milk

Do you see what I mean? I can't even pronounce half of those ingredients in margarine! While some people swear by salted butter, I would advise using unsalted butter so you can control the amount of salt yourself. The temperature and consistency of butter also plays an important part, depending on what you're making. Some recipes specifically require cold butter, in which case it's used straight from the refrigerator, however, for buttercream, soft butter is crucial in order to achieve that perfectly creamy texture. Most of my recipes require room temperature butter. Room temperature in the UK can be very different to room temperature elsewhere in a hotter or colder climate. Get to know your environment and how to achieve the perfect butter consistency for your purposes.

Flour

The invention of self-raising flour has saved you the job of weighing out your own raising agent, so it would be a crime not to take advantage of this! If you're feeling old school, or have no access to self-raising flour, replacing 5% of the flour with baking powder creates the same results. For example, 100g self-raising flour = 95g of plain flour + 5g of baking powder.

Another time-saving trick is to eradicate the sifting of flour. Rumour has it that back in the day when bakeries had large sacks of flour on the floor, mice and rats would tend to burrow their way in and do all sorts of nasty business there. The bakers would then have to sift the flour to make sure they removed any foreign objects before using it in recipes. Thankfully, the hygiene laws have improved for the better, so we no longer need to worry about finding a surprise in our flour. Therefore, there is no need to sift. It doesn't actually affect the fluffiness of the cake as that is a result of the raising agent, not the sifting.

Eggs

Eggs are one of the most versatile and intriguing ingredients available. There are countless ways to cook with eggs – poached or scrambled for breakfast, incorporated into savoury or sweet tart recipes, separated into the white and yolk to make meringues and pastry cream – the list is endless. Eggs play an important role in baking (and all cooking for that matter). They have a high protein content that helps bind ingredients and adds structure, so they are a necessity to most baked products.

If you're questioning why I'm weighing eggs rather than counting them, the answer is simple. You weigh every ingredient that goes into a recipe, so why wouldn't you weigh the eggs as well? If a recipe requires 6 eggs and each egg is overweight by 10g/¼oz, you could end up using a whole extra egg without realizing. This is crucial, especially if you're baking regularly and in large quantities and need consistent results.

Generally speaking, most recipes refer to large eggs unless stated otherwise. Another tip is to always weigh your eggs in a separate bowl before adding them to a batter or mixture to avoid any shell or bad eggs getting added to the mix. I also prefer using free-range fresh eggs and egg whites rather than cartoned ones (cartoned eggs/egg whites are chilled 'fresh' liquid eggs/egg whites that you can buy in cartons). Always keeping it fresh!

Please note that the weight of eggs given in all recipes is the weight without their shells.

Egg chart

Here's an eggs-tremely helpful lesson for you:

(Note: the weights shown below are for eggs without their shells)

Egg size	Small	Medium	Large
TOTAL WEIGHT	40g	50g	60g
YOLK	15g	20g	25g
WHITE	25g	30g	35g

The best way to separate an egg

1 Lightly tap the egg on the work surface or the bowl to crack the shell.

2 Hold the egg over a bowl and open up the egg into two parts, holding it upright, rather than sideways.

3 Allow the egg white to fall into the bowl underneath and catch the yolk in one half of the shell.

4 Pass the egg yolk to the other half of the shell, allowing more white to fall into the bowl.

5 Continue passing the yolk from one shell to the other until all the egg white has fallen into the bowl.

6 Place the egg yolk into a separate bowl.

Top Tip

If a piece of shell has fallen into the white, use one of the larger egg shell halves to take it out – the pieces of shell attract one another!

Sugar

Cakes (especially occasion cakes) are meant to be enjoyed in small quantities on special occasions and, therefore, sugar doesn't scare me. Cakes need sugar, otherwise, well, they're not cakes in my opinion! Not only does sugar give the cake the delicious sweetness that we all love, but it actually plays a part in the texture and moisture content of a sponge cake, too. I like to have access to all different kinds of sugars in my kitchen. Caster, granulated, icing, soft light/dark brown, demerara – they all have different purposes, different tastes and are used in different ways. Once again, baking is a science and altering the amount of sugar in a recipe can affect the end result.

Once you get over the fact that a large amount of sugar is usually used in baking, it's a fascinating ingredient. When mixed with a little water and heated in a pan, it can be used for making various different types of desserts. The subject of sugar would probably cover a book's worth of writing, but to introduce you to the exciting world of this sweet substance, I've written a guide below outlining the process of heating sugar.

As sugar heats up, the concentration of sugar increases and can be used in many different ways, depending on the stage it's heated up to. We're all familiar with caramel, the dark, rich sugary substance that gets stuck in your teeth. This is the furthest that sugar can get before burning, which means there are several more stages before it reaches caramel.

Firstly, sugar is very temperamental. It doesn't like being messed with, so when heating it up, as tempting as it is to mix it and fiddle with the thermometer, don't touch it. Otherwise, it can crystallize, which means the sugar seizes up and gets too hard and frosted to work with. Make sure you use a clean, heavy-based saucepan (which is not non-stick), as well as a clean sugar thermometer and a pastry brush with some extra water to wash down any stray sugar crystals from the sides of the saucepan when heating the sugar. Essentially, it doesn't matter how much water you add initially because water will start evaporating at 100°C/212°F. If you've put too much water in the saucepan, it will just take longer for the temperature to reach above 100°C/212°F. I usually add just enough water to cover the sugar in the saucepan.

Temperatures of sugar

When sugar reaches 107–110°C/225–230°F, it's referred to as the 'thread' stage. At this temperature, the sugar is more of a thick syrup. It's the same temperature used to make jam, which you will learn later on in the book.

At 116–120°C/241–248°F, the sugar reaches the 'soft ball' stage. This is the most commonly used stage throughout baking and we will use it in some of the recipes in this book.

Between 122–126°C/252–259°F, the sugar reaches the 'hard ball' stage. This is where the sugar concentration is quite high and can be used to make sweets such as gummies and nougat.

135°C/275°F is the 'crack' stage. This is the hardest stage of the sugar just before it turns to caramel. This sugar sets completely hard and can be used to make spun sugar, sugar sculptures, lollipops and pulled sugar (which is a much more technical process).

At 160°C/320°F, the sugar becomes darker in colour and turns to caramel. This is where all the water has completely evaporated and the sugar has become its most rich and concentrated state. At this temperature, the sugar is so hot that it will continue to cook itself, which is why you have to stop the heating process quickly by 'shocking' the pan by placing the bottom of the pan in a bowl of iced water. This caramel is used to top off desserts, coat in nuts and make brittle from. We will later be learning how to make a delicious caramel sauce to flavour cakes, which is a different process and recipe altogether.

Vanilla

Vanilla is a beautiful flavour and it's so versatile, but it can be pricey. My advice is to either purchase vanilla pods online in bulk or use a good-quality vanilla paste. An easy way of telling whether a paste is good quality is by looking to see if it contains tiny black dots of vanilla, then you know it's the real deal. Vanilla powder (see right) or good-quality vanilla extract are both good alternatives to vanilla paste. Stay away from vanilla 'essence' or 'flavouring' as they don't produce the same results and quite simply aren't as tasty. Remember, taste is key.

I tend to use vanilla powder or vanilla paste for my Ultimate Sponge Cake recipe (see page 30), then I prefer to use vanilla paste in my buttercream recipes, otherwise the vanilla powder will affect the texture of the buttercream.

To use a fresh vanilla pod, it needs to be cut open lengthways to reveal the abundance of flavourful seeds in the middle. Often, the skins go to waste, however, it's the skins that have the most flavour! So, I have a few tricks to reuse the skins and make the most of the vanilla pod:

Vanilla Sugar

Clean and sterilize an airtight container such as a clip-top jar.

Empty a bag of caster sugar into the jar along with a used (split) vanilla pod.

Seal the jar shut and keep it somewhere cool and dry.

Over time the vanilla will flavour the sugar to use in baking or even your cup of tea!

Vanilla Powder

Preheat the oven to 100°C/80°C fan/just below gas ¼.

Take a few used (split) vanilla pods and lay them on a baking tray.

Dry them in the oven for about 30 minutes.

Take them out and leave to cool completely.

Using a blender (like a smoothie blender), grind up the baked pods until a fine powder is formed.

Tip into an airtight container and store in a cool, dry place.

Add a sprinkling to cake batters for a fragrant vanilla flavour (see my Ultimate Sponge Cake recipe on page 30).

Vanilla Syrup

Later in the book you will learn how to make your own sugar syrup to soak your cakes in. Instead of using paste and extract, add a used vanilla pod to the sugar syrup for added flavour!

Chocolate

Chocolate comes in various forms: confectioner's bars, cooking slabs, chunks and chips. I prefer using chocolate chips because they have a smaller surface area and therefore melt down most efficiently. When it comes to working with chocolate, it's best to use couverture chocolate/chocolate chips. Couverture may sound like an intimidating word, but all it means is that the chocolate has a higher percentage of cocoa butter and is therefore higher in quality (and much tastier!). Compound or confectioner's chocolates may be cheaper but are made using other fats such as vegetable oils, which affect the quality of the chocolate. Couverture chocolate also allows it to be tempered – a process of heating and cooling down the chocolate at specific temperatures in order for it to set shiny and not melt when handled.

I usually use unsweetened cocoa powder in my cakes and save chocolate for buttercreams and decorations. As always, the better tasting the chocolate, the better tasting your cake will be so, if you can, try and use a high quality chocolate such as Belgian or Swiss. Chocolate also comes in different percentages of cocoa which affects the taste and behaviour of the chocolate. Higher percentages have less sugar and tend to be more bitter, whereas lower percentages have more sugar and sometimes the addition of milk and therefore are much sweeter. Chocolate also has various fat contents and therefore works in different ways (which we will cover later on in the book). My personal favourite chocolate to use is Callebaut's 54.5%. I think the balance of sweetness to bitterness is perfect and is beautiful to work with (… and eat!).

Baking terms and techniques

I've been in the baking world for over 10 years and so specific equipment and baking terms are second nature to me. To someone who has never baked before, certain terms may be unfamiliar. There is certain terminology that is specifically related to baking and cake decorating, so it's important that you understand exactly what they mean and what they entail.

Processes

BAIN-MARIE Used to melt ingredients gradually using a heatproof bowl sitting over a pan of gently simmering water. In my opinion, it's a myth that you shouldn't let the simmering water touch the bottom of the bowl when using a bain-marie for things like reheating ganache and melting chocolate.

BEAT Mixing ingredients at a high speed, usually using a beater attachment on a stand mixer.

BOIL Bringing a liquid to boiling point where vigorous bubbles appear (water boils at 100°C/212°F).

CREAM Softening a solid fat such as butter on a high speed, usually mixed with sugar to create a light and fluffy texture.

FOLD A term used to describe combining a lighter ingredient with a heavier one, such as flour into a cake batter. Using a spatula, turn over the ingredients gently rather than mixing them together vigorously.

SIFT Passing ingredients through a sieve to ensure there are no lumps remaining.

SIMMER Bringing a liquid to a temperature just below boiling where small bubbles begin to form (roughly 75°C/167°F).

WHISK Incorporating air using a hand whisk or whisk attachment on a stand mixer.

Oven settings

CONVENTIONAL This is where heat will be generated by elements in the top and bottom of the oven. The heat remains steady throughout the baking process. It's best to use one shelf at a time to ensure even heat.

FAN/TURBO The heat in the oven comes from the back where the fan has its own heating mechanism and circulates heat around the oven. Good fan ovens will spread heat evenly, which means you can use multiple trays at the same time, however, some ovens may require for the trays or cakes to be turned during the baking process. Fan temperatures are typically set 20°C lower than conventional oven temperatures.

Cake terms

BATTER a mixture of flour and other ingredients used to make baked goods.

LAYER A cake is made up of layers of sponge sandwiched together with layers of buttercream.

STACKING The process of either placing a layer of cake onto a layer of buttercream or placing a tier of cake onto a larger tier of cake.

TIER A level of a cake. A single tier is usually one size of cake, multiple tiers consist of different-sized cakes stacked on top of each other.

MAKING THE SPONGE

The foundation to any show-stopping cake is, well, the cake. Starting off with a sturdy cake that is suitable for stacking cakes is a must. Sturdy doesn't have to mean dry and underwhelming either. I have developed a recipe that is not only delicious but is also perfect for layering and stacking buttercream cakes. Before the baking commences, I'm going to guide you through the preparations and necessities for baking your sponge to perfection.

A guide to perfectly cooked sponge

Perfecting your sponge cake is critical. There are tons of recipes incorporating all sorts of ingredients, such as yogurt, buttermilk, oils, etc, and some people swear by their own recipes, which is totally fine! However, my recipe not only contains simple and regular ingredients, but it also keeps clear of any confusing processes and misleading instructions. After all, a cake needs to taste just as good as it looks.

The reason why baking can seem like such a daunting and scary task is because our heads have been filled with old wives' tales and myths of what to do and what not to do in order to achieve a perfect bake. Throughout my experience of baking on both small and (very) large scales, I quickly discovered exactly which rules to follow and which were a load of nonsense. There's no denying that one has to be careful and precise when baking, but you can relax more than you think, which also makes the experience a lot more enjoyable!

Baking myths explained

MYTH #1 *"DON'T OPEN THE OVEN DOOR WHILE BAKING"*
Agree... to an extent. Opening the door of the oven lets in cooler air and can therefore affect the temperature inside the oven. However, if you're careful and if it's for a few seconds, then it's fine to open the oven door. What is crucial to avoid is slamming the door shut, as this sudden jolt can interfere with the rising of the cake and could even cause the cake to sink. Most ovens have a 'hot spot' either at the front or back and therefore it is vital to rotate the cake halfway or two-thirds of the way through baking. So if anything, you should open the oven door at least once to maintain an even bake... just be careful with the door!

MYTH #2 *"INSERT A KNIFE/SKEWER TO CHECK IF A CAKE IS COOKED. IF IT COMES OUT CLEAN THEN THE CAKE IS READY"*
Disagree. When I started baking, I used to test my cakes in this way and once the cakes were cool, a little sunken dip usually appeared in the centre. This is the most common sign of under-baking. I decided that this knife/skewer technique wasn't the most accurate, so from then on I decided to use my baker's instinct over the knife/skewer test. When you think the cake is baked, touch the top and press it down slightly. If it feels foamy and soft inside, it's not baked. If it feels like there is a slight resistance and bounce-back when you press it, then it's ready and can come out of the oven. Those extra 5 minutes are so crucial, so much so I prefer leaving the cake in for extra time just to be sure... which leads me onto...

MYTH #3 *"TIMING IS ESSENTIAL; A MINUTE OVER AND YOUR BAKE IS RUINED"*
Timing is essential, but it depends on what you are baking. Generally speaking, the shorter cooking time needed in the oven, the more precise you have to be. Pastries, biscuits and cookies only need about 10–15 minutes in the oven, so it's easier to overbake them, even by 1 minute; however, meringues and cakes are more lenient. As mentioned above, I would much rather leave a cake in for 2 minutes longer than the risk of having an undercooked sponge. Always set a timer in any case!

Lining a cake tin

In order to achieve a perfect bake, you need to do things correctly from the start. If your cake tin isn't lined properly, you run the risk of the sponge sticking to the tin. Some people swear by 'cake release spray' and while it may work wonders, when I have tried it in the past, I felt that it coated the lining of my mouth and lungs as well as the tin, so I'd rather just avoid it. There is always butter and oil in my kitchen, so instead of purchasing an extra product, I would rather use what I already have to grease the cake tins.

1 Brush a small amount of melted or softened butter all over the inside of each cake tin, sides and bottom.

2 Take a large piece of baking paper and fold it in half (make sure the paper is now the same size as one cake tin).

3 Fold the paper in half again, horizontally. There should now be two edges which are folded, and two that are open.

4 Where the open and folded edges meet, bring those corners of paper together so you get a triangle shape (don't worry if they don't meet up exactly).

5 Repeat this step to make a narrower triangle (the point of the triangle should be closed).

6 Place the triangle over the cake tin, roughly measure the radius and trim the end of the paper triangle with scissors.

7 Open out the paper and you should have two circles which match the size of the two cake tins. Place a circle of paper at the bottom of each tin.

8 Use scraps of baking paper or ready-cut strips to line the sides of the tin. Make sure that no part of the tin is showing as this will catch the cake. Once the cake is cooked and removed from the tins, this paper comes away very easily.

3

4

5

6

7

8

The ultimate sponge cake recipe

I like to call this recipe the 'One Pan Band', as you can quite literally create the sponge in one saucepan – meaning less washing up, too! This is one of the most simple cake recipes you will ever make *and* it's absolutely delicious. The reason why I melt butter in my recipe is that I always heard the secret to a moist cake is the use of oil. Certain oils aren't meant to be cooked over certain temperatures, so I thought to myself, "How can I achieve the same effect without using oil?" *Light-bulb moment* Let's try melting the butter instead.

The first time I made this recipe, the cake came out perfectly. This technique also eliminates creaming the butter and sugar, which can lead to it clumping together, forming uneven patches in your sponge. This cake batter comes together so smoothly and therefore cooks much more evenly.

YOU WILL NEED
two 15cm/6in round cake tins (each at least 7.5cm/3in deep)
medium saucepan
whisk
rubber spatula

INGREDIENTS
250g/9oz/generous 1 cup unsalted butter, plus extra for greasing
250g/9oz/1¼ cups caster sugar
½ tsp vanilla powder or vanilla paste
200g/7oz eggs
250g/9oz/scant 2 cups self-raising flour (or *238g/8½oz/1¾ cups plain flour and 12g/¼oz baking powder sifted together*)

1 Preheat the oven to 180°C/160°C fan/gas 4.

2 Grease and line your two cake tins and set them aside (see page 28 for the best lining techniques).

3 In a saucepan, gently melt the butter over a low heat to avoid it bubbling. Once melted, remove the pan from the heat, add in the caster sugar with the vanilla and use a whisk to combine until fully incorporated and a thick paste has formed.

4 Lightly beat the eggs in a bowl or jug, then add to the butter and sugar and mix until fully incorporated.

5 Swap your whisk for a spatula and fold in the flour until a smooth batter has formed.

6 Weigh out half of the batter (roughly 470g/1lb 1oz) into each lined tin and level the surface.

Photo Steps Continue Overleaf _____

6

8

7 Bake for 40–45 minutes until the sponges are cooked all the way through.

8 Take out of the oven and leave to cool in the tins for about 5 minutes.

9 Pop the cakes out of the tins by pushing up from the

bottom with your hand, remove the baking paper and leave on a wire rack until cooled completely.

10 Wrap the sponges in clingfilm or place them in an airtight container overnight until you are ready to fill and decorate them.

Top Tips

• Sponges freeze very well. If you want to bake your sponges in advance, wrap them in clingfilm and freeze them for up to 3 months. Leave at room temperature to defrost.

• Never put a sponge in the refrigerator. It will dry the sponge out. Later on in the book you will find out at which stage you can keep a cake in the refrigerator.

• If your cake is doming too much, your oven temperature is too high. Turn the temperature down 5–10°C to avoid this from happening.

Multiplying the recipe for larger cakes

I always get asked how to adapt my recipe for larger cakes. My Ultimate Sponge Cake recipe is easy to multiply and, unlike some other recipes, creating a larger volume doesn't have an effect on the results. My recipe can also be used for any size or shaped cake tin – it really is that versatile!

Note: *When I refer to a 'batch', I'm referring to my recipe mix of 250g/9oz/generous 1 cup of butter, 250g/9oz/1¼ cups caster sugar, etc, from my ultimate recipe on page 30.*

Square tins

Square cake tins have a larger volume so multiply the original recipe by 1.5

 = BATCH   = FEEDS

2 × 15CM/6IN TINS =	2 × 20CM/8IN TINS =	2 × 25CM/10IN TINS =	2 × 30CM/12IN TINS =
1	3	4.5	6
20-25	50-60	80-90	120-140

375g/13oz/scant 1¾ cups unsalted butter	750g/1lb 10oz/3⅓ cups unsalted butter	1125g/2lb 7¾oz/5 cups unsalted butter	1500g/3lb 5oz/6¾ cups unsalted butter
375g/13oz/scant 2 cups caster sugar	750g/1lb 10oz/3¾ cups caster sugar	1125g/2lb 7¾oz/5⅔ cups caster sugar	1500g/3lb 5oz/7½ cups caster sugar
½ tsp vanilla powder or vanilla paste	1 tsp vanilla powder or vanilla paste	1½ tsp vanilla powder or vanilla paste	2 tsp vanilla powder or vanilla paste
300g/10½oz eggs	600g/1lb 5oz eggs	900g/2lb eggs	1200g/2lb 10oz eggs
375g/13oz/generous 2¾ cups self-raising flour (or 357g/12¼oz/2¾ cups plain flour and 18g/¾oz baking powder sifted together)	750g/1lb 10oz/5⅔ cups self-raising flour (or 714g/1lb 9½oz/generous 5⅓ cups plain flour and 36g/1¼oz baking powder sifted together)	1125g/2lb 7¾oz/8½ cups self-raising flour (or 1071g/2lb 6oz/8 cups plain flour and 54g/2oz baking powder sifted together)	1500g/3lb 5oz/11¼ cups self-raising flour (or 1428g/3lb 2oz/10¾ cups plain flour and 72g/2½oz baking powder sifted together)
Bake for 50–55 minutes.	Bake for 55–60 minutes.	Bake for 65–70 minutes.	Bake for 70–75 minutes. and so on.

Round tins

2 × 15CM/6IN TINS = 1

15-20

250g/9oz/generous 1 cup unsalted butter
250g/9oz/1¼ cups caster sugar
½ tsp vanilla powder or vanilla paste
200g/7oz eggs
250g/9oz/scant 2 cups self-raising flour (or 238g/8½oz/1¾ cups plain flour and 12g/¼oz baking powder sifted together)

Bake for 40–45 minutes.

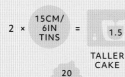

2 × 15CM/6IN TINS = 1.5

TALLER CAKE

20-25

375g/13oz/scant 1¾ cups unsalted butter
375g/13oz/scant 2 cups caster sugar
½ tsp vanilla powder or vanilla paste
300g/10½oz eggs
375g/13oz/generous 2¾ cups self-raising flour (or 357g/12¼oz/2¾ cups plain flour and 18g/¾oz baking powder sifted together)

Bake for 50–55 minutes.

2 × 20CM/8IN TINS = 2

35-40

500g/1lb 2oz/scant 2¼ cups unsalted butter
500g/1lb 2oz/2½ cups caster sugar
½ tsp vanilla powder or vanilla paste
400g/14oz eggs
500g/1lb 2oz/3¾ cups self-raising flour (or 476g/1lb 1oz/3½ cups plain flour and 24g/1oz baking powder sifted together)

Bake for 50–55 minutes.

2 × 25CM/10IN TINS = 3

50-60

750g/1lb 10oz/3⅓ cups unsalted butter
750g/1lb 10oz/3¾ cups caster sugar
1 tsp vanilla powder or vanilla paste
600g/1lb 5oz eggs
750g/1lb 10oz/5⅔ cups self-raising flour (or 714g/1lb 9½oz/generous 5⅓ cups plain flour and 36g/1¼oz baking powder sifted together)

Bake for 60–65 minutes.

2 × 30CM/12IN TINS = 4

70-80

1kg/2lb 4oz/generous 4½ cups unsalted butter
1kg/2lb 4oz/5 cups caster sugar
1 tsp vanilla powder or vanilla paste
800g/1lb 12oz eggs
1kg/2lb 4oz/7½ cups self-raising flour (or 952g/2lb 2oz/7 cups plain flour and 48g/1¾oz baking powder sifted together)

Bake for 65–70 minutes.

AND SO ON. IT IS ALSO POSSIBLE TO ADAPT THE RECIPE FOR SMALLER TINS, TOO, SUCH AS A 10CM/4IN CAKE. SEE THE TWO EXAMPLES TO THE RIGHT.

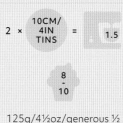

2 × 10CM/4IN TINS = 1.5

8-10

125g/4½oz/generous ½ cup unsalted butter
125g/4½oz/⅔ cup caster sugar
¼ tsp vanilla powder or vanilla paste
100g/3½oz eggs
125g/4½oz/scant 1 cup self-raising flour (or 119g/4¼oz/scant 1 cup plain flour and 6g/⅛oz baking powder sifted together)

Bake for 30–35 minutes.

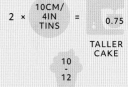

2 × 10CM/4IN TINS = 0.75

TALLER CAKE

10-12

190g/6¾oz/generous ¾ cup unsalted butter
190g/6¾oz/scant 1 cup caster sugar
½ tsp vanilla powder or vanilla paste
150g/5½oz eggs
190g/6¾oz/scant 1½ cups self-raising flour (or 181g/6¼oz/1⅓ cups plain flour and 9g/¼oz baking powder sifted together)

Bake for 40–45 minutes.

Flavouring the sponge

We've covered how to adapt the sponge recipe for larger quantities, now let's talk about flavour. I'm always surprised by how many cake recipes there are out there. At the end of the day, a cake is made up of the same ingredients with a few alterations and extra ingredients here and there. My cake recipe is a great foundation for a sponge and can be adapted and flavoured in many ways. Baking is a scientific formula, so as long as you keep all the aspects in proportion, you're guaranteed a perfect bake every time. As always, flavour is just as important as the look of the cake, so make sure you're using as higher quality ingredients as possible. After all, the better the ingredients, the better tasting the cake!

Over the next few pages you will find some of my favourite cake flavours and easy ways to adapt the sponge cake.

Lemon sponge

When I eat a lemon cake I want it to be singing with lemon flavour. Not just a subtle hint, I want an explosion in my mouth. I love pairing my lemon sponge cake up with a lemon soaking syrup, lemon curd and vanilla buttercream, which you'll learn about in the coming chapters.

INGREDIENTS
250g/9oz/generous 1 cup unsalted butter
250g/9oz/1¼ cups caster sugar
½ tsp vanilla powder or vanilla paste
200g/7oz eggs
250g/9oz/scant 2 cups self-raising flour
    (or 238g/8½oz/1¾ cups plain flour and 12g/¼oz
    baking powder sifted together)
finely grated zest of 2 large lemons

Follow the same method as the original recipe (see page 30).

Add the lemon zest after you have added and incorporated the flour into the mix. Stir to combine.

Raspberry sponge

This recipe can be adapted using any frozen berries, whether it's blueberries or strawberries; however, there's something about the tartness of raspberries that I just love. Plus, I feel raspberries have the perfect texture to mix into a cake batter, as other fruits can be a little too watery and therefore can affect the texture of the cake too much. Adding some lemon zest to this recipe gives it an extra kick.

INGREDIENTS
250g/9oz/generous 1 cup unsalted butter
250g/9oz/1¼ cups caster sugar
½ tsp vanilla powder or vanilla paste
200g/7oz eggs
100g/3½oz frozen raspberries
250g/9oz/scant 2 cups self-raising flour
    (or 238g/8½oz/1¾ cups plain flour and 12g/¼oz
    baking powder sifted together)
finely grated zest of 1 lemon (optional)

Follow the same method as the original recipe (see page 30). Toss the raspberries in a light dusting of the measured flour (about 1 tablespoon) before adding them to the batter after incorporating the remaining flour. If using lemon zest, add it in with the flour.

Coffee sponge

It's hard to say which flavour of cake is my favourite, but coffee has to be one of them. Coffee cake is the perfect balance of sweetness and flavour and can be paired with chocolate buttercream, coffee buttercream, even some extra nuts thrown in, too. Soaking this cake with coffee syrup really takes it to another level.

INGREDIENTS
250g/9oz/generous 1 cup unsalted butter
250g/9oz/1¼ cups soft light brown sugar
60ml/4 tbsp/¼ cup espresso
½ tsp vanilla powder or vanilla paste
200g/7oz eggs
250g/9oz/scant 2 cups self-raising flour
    (or 238g/8½oz/1¾ cups plain flour and 12g/¼oz baking
    powder sifted together)
100g/3½oz roughly chopped pecans or walnuts (optional)

Follow the same method as the original recipe (see page 30), adding the espresso in with the melted butter and sugar. If adding nuts, fold them in at the end after the flour is incorporated.

Chocolate sponge

I always say that when it comes to decorating a cake with layers of buttercream, it's hard to get a real muddy melt-in-the-mouth chocolate cake, mainly because the cake has to be able to support itself. Rich and dense chocolate cakes can be too soft; however, this recipe is stable enough for stacked cakes, yet is still moist and chocolatey enough for chocolate lovers.

INGREDIENTS
250g/9oz/generous 1 cup unsalted butter
250g/9oz/1¼ cups caster sugar
½ tsp vanilla powder or vanilla paste
200g/7oz eggs
200g/7oz/1½ cups self-raising flour (or 190g/6¾oz/
    scant 1½ cups plain flour and 10g/¼oz baking powder
    sifted together)
50g/1¾oz/½ cup good-quality unsweetened cocoa
    powder
5g/⅛oz bicarbonate of soda
200g/7oz/scant 1 cup natural yogurt

Follow the same method as the original recipe (see page 30), just sift the flour, cocoa powder and bicarb together. Add in the yogurt at the end and stir to combine.

You will notice that I added a couple more ingredients to this cake. Cocoa powder has a very dry texture and absorbs a lot of the moisture in a cake. To balance out the moisture of the cake, I like to add yogurt. This adds in more moisture and maintains that indulgent chocolate taste, too. The bicarbonate of soda is there to maximize the rise of the cake, too, because it's a heavier sponge due to the cocoa.

Top Tip

Toss the nuts in a light dusting of the measured flour before adding to the batter – this will help prevent them from sinking to the bottom of the cake!

Sugar soaking syrup

Sugar syrup is something you may have never used before when making a cake, but it's one of my finest tricks. The one thing that we all want to avoid when making a cake is serving a dry sponge. Sugar syrup, also known as sugar soaking syrup, prevents dryness and can even enhance flavour, too. It's an extremely simple recipe, easy to adapt by adding different flavours, and makes such a difference to the taste and shelf life of your cake.

Over the page is my easily adaptable recipe and how I like to use and store it.

YOU WILL NEED
heatproof container or small saucepan
pastry brush or soaking bottle

Each syrup recipe makes enough to soak 4 layers of one 15cm/6in cake

Simple vanilla syrup

INGREDIENTS
50g/1¾oz/¼ cup caster sugar
50ml/1¾fl oz boiling water
1 used vanilla pod skin or a drop of vanilla paste

1 Measure out the caster sugar in a heatproof container and place back onto the measuring scales.

2 Pour over the boiling water, measuring the 50ml/1¾fl oz as you pour.

3 Stir with a metal spoon to dissolve the sugar.

4 Add the vanilla (pod or paste) and mix until you can see the little specks of vanilla in the syrup. If using a vanilla pod, you can leave the vanilla pod in the syrup.

5 Leave the syrup to cool down completely before use.

6 Apply the sugar soaking syrup to your cake using a pastry brush or a soaking syrup bottle (see page 46).

Depending on the flavour of the cake you're making, you can adjust the syrup recipe by swapping the water for another liquid to enhance that particular flavour.

Citrus syrup

INGREDIENTS
50ml/1¾fl oz freshly squeezed citrus juice
    (e.g. lemon, lime or orange)
50g/1¾oz/¼ cup caster sugar

1 Place both the citrus juice and sugar into a small saucepan.

2 Stir the mixture over a low heat until all the sugar has dissolved.

3 Keep heating until it just comes to the boil and then take off the heat and leave to cool completely before use.

4 Apply the sugar soaking syrup to your cake using a pastry brush or a soaking syrup bottle (see page 46).

Honey syrup

INGREDIENTS
50g/1¾oz runny honey
50ml/1¾fl oz boiling water

1 Measure out the honey in a heatproof container and place back onto the measuring scales.

2 Pour over the boiling water, measuring the 50ml/1¾fl oz as you pour.

3 Stir with a metal spoon to dissolve the honey, and leave the syrup to cool down completely before use.

4 Apply the sugar soaking syrup to your cake using a pastry brush or a soaking syrup bottle (see page 46).

Coffee syrup

INGREDIENTS
50ml/1¾fl oz espresso, made using hot water
50g/1¾oz/¼ cup caster sugar

1 While the coffee is still hot, add in the sugar and stir to dissolve. Leave to cool completely.

2 If the sugar hasn't dissolved completely, heat it up in a small saucepan until the sugar has dissolved, then cool completely before use.

3 Apply the sugar soaking syrup to your cake using a pastry brush or a soaking syrup bottle (see page 46).

Soaking syrup bottle

The obvious way to apply the syrup would be to use a pastry brush; however, I find that the brushes with hair tend to leave bristles over the sponge, which is something we definitely want to avoid, and the silicone brushes don't pick up enough liquid at a time, so, here is an easy DIY trick to apply syrup.

1 Wash out a used small plastic bottle (with a capacity of at least 100ml/3½fl oz/scant ½ cup).

2 Poke a few holes in the bottle's cap using a drawing pin or needle.

3 Wait until the sugar syrup has cooled down completely, then fill the bottle with the syrup. If you have used a vanilla pod, place the pod in the bottle before you pour in the syrup.

4 Place the cap back on the bottle and turn the bottle upside down to pour the syrup over the cakes.

Storage

I usually make the sugar soaking syrup fresh every time as I make different cakes all the time. However, the syrups can all be made in advance and stored (once cooled) in the soaking syrup bottle or in an airtight container in the refrigerator for up to 2 weeks.

BUTTERCREAM & FILLINGS

Cake decorating has completely modernized over the last few years. Gone are the days of dense fruit cake, marzipan and fondant icing that is too sickly to eat. Personally, I think that the beauty of a cake is that everything on it is edible and, more importantly, enjoyable to eat. I don't want to peel off icing before I take a bite into a cake!

Buttercream took centre stage when people realized that it was more than just a filling, but can also be used to decorate the outside of the cake. When I made my first few cakes, I used 'American frosting' buttercream, made of just butter and icing sugar. I found it very sweet and, while it did the job, I wasn't happy with the results when I used it for stacking and decorating cakes. The buttercream was far too dense and sickly for a multi-layered cake and I also found that I never achieved a flawless smooth finish on the outside of a cake. Luckily, I came across Swiss meringue buttercream and, once I got the hang of it, I never looked back.

SWISS MERINGUE BUTTERCREAM

51

FRENCH BUTTERCREAM

58

CHOCOLATE GANACHE

62

JAM

68

CURD

72

SALTED CARAMEL

76

Swiss meringue buttercream

You can probably tell by the name that this buttercream has a meringue base. It sounded strange to me at first, but after using it, I was totally converted and it made my cakes look and taste better. While this buttercream has a softer finish and doesn't crust or set like American frosting does, it is actually much stronger and holds the cake up for a lot longer. This is due to the protein in the egg whites that are used in the recipe.

The recipe of Swiss meringue is made from one part egg whites and two parts sugar. To turn the meringue into a buttercream, the same amount of butter as the sugar is added at the end. It's as simple as that.

The process, however, is not so simple. This buttercream does take a little longer to make and is more technical, too. Luckily for you, I now know every trick in the book to avoid a Swiss meringue buttercream catastrophe, so you can make it time and time again without any mishaps!

Here are a few top tips to keep in mind when making Swiss meringue buttercream:

USE FRESH EGG WHITES: In the past, I've tried using cartoned egg whites (chilled 'fresh' liquid egg whites that you can buy in cartons) because I hated the idea of wasting so many of the yolks. However, cartoned egg whites usually contain other ingredients such as stabilizers, which affects the result of the meringue. The meringue simply does not whisk up to a stiff enough consistency and therefore I only ever use fresh egg whites that I've separated myself (see page 17 for the best way to separate an egg). If you don't like the idea of wasting the yolks, there are plenty of recipes that use just egg yolks (including the next recipe in this book!).

Separated egg whites and egg yolks can be stored in airtight containers or covered bowls in the refrigerator for up to 2 days.

Fresh egg whites also freeze very well in an airtight container for up to 2 months. I like to defrost the egg whites in the refrigerator overnight. You can also freeze egg yolks; however, during the freezing process, their texture changes. Combine the egg yolks with a little bit of caster sugar before freezing them in an airtight container. The sugar will help bring the yolks back to their original texture once defrosted. Yolks can also be stored in the freezer for up to 2 months.

TRY TO ALWAYS MAKE IT FRESH: This buttercream works best when it's been made fresh. Even though planning ahead and being organized is a big part of the cake decorating process, it's more work bringing the buttercream back to spreadable consistency having kept it in the refrigerator/freezer, then making it from scratch. I will explain how to bring it back in this chapter if you do need to make it in advance, but I highly recommend making it fresh every time.

BE AWARE OF HOW MUCH YOUR MIXER CAN HOLD AT ONE TIME: The way the buttercream forms is all about whisking in specific amounts of air once the butter has been added. If the mixer bowl is too full, the air won't incorporate properly and therefore the buttercream won't form. Later on I will explain the different amounts of buttercream for different-sized cakes and mixers.

BE PATIENT AND BELIEVE IN THE PROCESS: As I mentioned earlier, this buttercream takes longer to make than regular buttercream but it is totally worth it. Working with a smoother buttercream leads to better results and therefore you can be more efficient with your time management and be a much happier baker by the end of it!

Swiss meringue buttercream recipe

This makes enough to fill, stack and decorate a 15cm/6in cake.
It can be made in a standard-sized stand mixer.

YOU WILL NEED
stand mixer with whisk attachment
heatproof rubber spatula
pan of simmering water
sugar thermometer

INGREDIENTS
200g/7oz egg whites
400g/14oz/2 cups caster sugar
400g/14oz/1¾ cups unsalted butter at room temperature, cut into cubes

1 Place the egg whites and sugar in a stand mixer bowl and mix together using a rubber spatula until you can't see any more strands of egg white and it's fully combined with the sugar. Use the spatula to clean the sides of the bowl of any sugar and egg white that's crept up the sides.

2 Place the bowl over a pan of gently simmering water (bain-marie) and continue to stir with the spatula to maintain an even temperature throughout.

It's important that the pan is simmering rather than boiling as we now want to melt the sugar into the egg whites gradually.

3 Continue stirring and cleaning the sides of the bowl from any sugar grains that have come up the sides.

4 Once it starts to feel loose, you can start taking the temperature of the mix.

Keep mixing while holding the thermometer in place to make sure you're getting an even reading, otherwise it will only read one part.

5 Heat until it reaches 65°C/149°F and then take the bowl off the water.

Because we're making buttercream and not baking this meringue, we need to cook the eggs so they're

safe to eat. Eggs pasteurize at 63°C/145°F, but I like taking it to 65°C/149°F just to be on the safe side.

6 Make sure all the sugar has dissolved into the egg whites, so clean around the sides of the bowl one more time using the rubber spatula.

Make sure that there are no sugar crystals left on the side of the bowl, as these can create unwanted sugar crystals in your buttercream, which may affect the final finish of buttercream on your cake.

7 Place onto the stand mixer and whisk at full speed for at least 5 minutes until a thick meringue has formed. You're looking for extremely stiff peaks with the meringue, where you can see defined trails of the whisk while it's mixing and the meringue doesn't move once it's stopped whisking.

8 Once the meringue has formed, stop the mixer and lift up the head of the mixer.

If the meringue has cooled after 5 minutes, then you can skip straight to adding the butter. I turn off the mixer at this stage purely because I don't like having the mixer on a high speed for too long!

Photo Steps Continue Overleaf _____

9 Leave the meringue standing to cool completely.

IMPORTANT: If the butter is added when the bowl is still warm, the butter will melt and the buttercream won't come together properly.

10 When the mixer bowl has cooled to room temperature, turn the mixer onto a medium speed and slowly add the pieces of softened butter, one cube at a time.

I like adding the butter by hand so I can give the butter an extra squash if needed. It's also important to feel the texture of your butter – if it's quite soft, you can add it quicker, if it's still a bit firm, squeeze it in your fingers before adding it to the meringue.

11 Once all the butter is inside the meringue, leave the mixer on a medium speed.

Moment of truth!

12 While it may look like nothing is happening at this moment, the edges of the meringue will start looking a bit grainy, as if you've over mixed it, but don't worry! This is the sign that it's working.

Most people see the mixture 'splitting' and freak out. This is a GOOD SIGN! It means it's working!

13 Continue mixing on the same speed and eventually the meringue around the edges starts to catch around the whisk and the meringue starts to thicken in the centre.

14 Once it has thickened and starts pulling away from the sides, turn the speed up to maximum to whisk in the remaining meringue and any leftover butter lumps.

15 Mix on a high speed for about 30 seconds and then turn the mixer off completely.

16 Take the bowl from the mixer and use a rubber spatula to scrape around the sides of the bowl and mix the buttercream by hand to make sure everything has incorporated.

Mixing by hand at this stage also knocks out air bubbles, which will make your buttercream smoother.

17 Your Swiss meringue buttercream is now ready to flavour!

Flavouring your Swiss meringue buttercream

You've made this beautiful, glossy buttercream that tastes like marshmallow even without adding flavour, but the beauty of this buttercream is that it's very adaptable and can hold pretty much any flavour! The amount that was made in the previous recipe is enough to fill, stack and decorate a 15cm/6in cake, so bear this in mind when flavouring your buttercream. Adding certain flavours will, of course, alter the colour of the buttercream. If I want to add a flavour which will alter the colour of the buttercream, I divide the buttercream into two bowls and add whichever flavour I'm using to one half while keep the remaining half naturally white so I can colour it afterwards to use for the outside of the cake.

Vanilla

In most of the cakes that I make, I flavour the buttercream with vanilla paste. Half a teaspoon of vanilla paste mixed into this buttercream really enhances the marshmallowy flavour, and even works if you then add an additional flavour, too. I love seeing the little black dots of the vanilla dispersed in the buttercream, it makes it even more appetizing as you know it's going to taste really good!

Chocolate

When chocolate is added to this buttercream, it ends up tasting like silky chocolate mousse. The type of chocolate that is added to the buttercream will determine the amount needed. Generally speaking, the darker the chocolate, the richer the taste. For dark chocolate (70–90% cocoa solids), I would add 100–150g/3½–5½oz to the basic recipe. For milk and even white chocolate, I would add 150–200g/ 5½–7oz. When adding a flavour, I add it in stages so I can taste it along the way. If I've added 150g/5½oz of white chocolate and I think it tastes chocolatey enough, then I won't add more; however, sometimes I think it needs more of a kick so will add the remaining 50g/1¾oz.

To add chocolate to the buttercream, it needs to be melted. Melted chocolate gets warm and therefore has to cool down to room temperature before adding it to the buttercream. If you pour in warm chocolate, you'll get chocolate soup, which is what we want to avoid. The best way of melting chocolate is resting a heatproof bowl over a pan of gently simmering water and allowing the chocolate to slowly melt in the bowl. You can also melt chocolate in the microwave in short bursts of 20–30 seconds at a time (I usually do this on high/full power, but microwave ovens vary, so adjust the setting used to suit your model; when working with chocolate, it's always better to err on the safe side). Any longer and the chocolate can easily burn. Leave the melted chocolate to cool completely. Once the chocolate has cooled (but not set), add it to the buttercream and fold it in using a spatula. Incorporating chocolate makes the buttercream silky smooth and sometimes a bit looser. This is where you have to be careful with the amount of chocolate you add, or any flavour for that matter, as you want to avoid making the buttercream too loose to handle.

Coffee

Just like a coffee sponge, coffee buttercream is one of my favourites. The contrast between the sour taste of coffee with the sweet buttercream is an absolute treat. Coffee is more liquid than chocolate is, therefore it needs whisking into the buttercream rather than folding in by hand. Due to the fat in the buttercream, if a liquid is added, the buttercream can separate. Whisking the liquid in on a high speed in the stand mixer will prevent that from happening.

I add an espresso shot (35ml/2⅓ tbsp) of coffee to my buttercream, as it's the strongest tasting form of coffee. Like the chocolate, wait for the coffee to cool down to room temperature before adding it to the buttercream, and the less added liquid the better. Start off with one shot, and if you think the coffee flavour needs to be stronger, then add another shot.

Fruit juice and purée

When I say fruit juice, I don't mean fruit juice in a carton. I'm referring to freshly squeezed juice from fresh raspberries, strawberries and blackberries (if using frozen fruit, allow it to defrost fully first before sieving). I pass about 100g/3½oz through a sieve, using a fork to extract the juice without the pips and pulp, and then add the juice to the buttercream. Not only does it flavour the buttercream wonderfully, the colour is just incredible. You can get natural pinks and purples just using this fruit. Ready-made fruit purées are another excellent way of adding flavour to the buttercream (and a lot less messy!). They're usually more concentrated, so start with 50g/1¾oz of purée and add more depending on the fruit and the taste.

Similar to coffee, juice is a liquid and therefore it's best to whisk the juice into the buttercream rather than fold it through.

Spreads

Whether it's peanut butter, hazelnut spread, speculoos or salted caramel, all spreads mix into buttercream seamlessly. The thicker consistency allows the spread to fully incorporate into the buttercream without it splitting. Depending on the spread you're using, 1–2 tablespoons is enough to flavour the buttercream. I love adding spreads as a flavour as it makes the cake more fun and kids love it, too!

What you will probably notice is that most of these flavours will affect the consistency of the buttercream. Sometimes for the better (smoother and less aerated) and sometimes it can get looser and therefore trickier to work with. Flavouring is something to get used to over time and familiarize yourself with, with the ingredients that you have access to. Experimenting with flavours is also part of the fun, so enjoy it and get creative!

How to store buttercream and bring it back to a spreadable consistency

Even though I prefer making my buttercream fresh every time, I understand that some people like to plan ahead and be as organized as possible. Even delegating a day just to make buttercream may save time in the long run. However, bringing it back to a spreadable and usable consistency is a process and takes time.

Buttercream can be stored in an airtight container in the refrigerator for up to a week and in the freezer for up to 3 months. When I have any left over, I usually place it in a small bowl and cover it with clingfilm, which also keeps it fresh.

Bringing buttercream back to a spreadable consistency involves taking the buttercream out of the refrigerator or freezer and leaving it at room temperature to become completely soft. The time for buttercream to soften can vary depending on the climate, time of year and how much buttercream there is. In the winter months, it can take up to 4 hours for the buttercream to soften, whereas in the summer it can soften within an hour, so you really need to understand and practise within the environment you're working in.

Once the buttercream has completely softened, it will need to be whisked using the stand mixer for about a minute to fully come back together. If there is still a hard piece of buttercream remaining, it can cause the buttercream to split when mixing up again, which is why it's so important for the buttercream to have softened completely.

As you can see, this is quite a lengthy process, which is why I prefer making my buttercream fresh. But it is possible!

Different buttercream quantities for different-sized mixers

As mentioned earlier, the process of making Swiss meringue buttercream involves incorporating air. While the recipe is easily adaptable for different amounts, the mixer bowl can only withstand a certain volume of buttercream. In addition, the buttercream won't work if there is not enough room for the air to incorporate either.

For a standard-sized mixer (4.73L/ 5 quarts), the maximum amount of buttercream that can be made is: 250g/9oz of egg whites, 500g/ 1lb 2oz/2½ cups of sugar and 500g/ 1lb 2oz/scant 2¼ cups of butter.

For a larger mixer (6.62L/7quarts), the maximum amount of buttercream that can be made is: 450g/1lb of egg whites, 900g/2lb/4½ cups of sugar and 900g/2lb/4 cups of butter.

My first ever mixer was actually the larger size. I decided to invest in it right at the beginning of my cake journey and I'm glad I did! It allowed me to make larger quantities at one time and therefore I was more efficient with my timing. If you're serious about baking, it's definitely worth the investment.

French buttercream

The reason why I like French buttercream is because it uses up the egg yolks that remain from the previous recipe! French buttercream is a bit denser and richer than Swiss meringue buttercream. Even though it works perfectly fine for decorating cakes, I love using this buttercream with smaller treats, such as filling macarons or topping cupcakes, because of its intensity. The method of this buttercream entails some technical steps, but it's harder to mess up! The process includes heating sugar syrup to a specific temperature to cook the egg yolks, rather than heating them up over a bain-marie like in the Swiss meringue buttercream recipe. When heating up sugar, it passes through multiple stages and is used for different purposes. To learn more about the temperature stages of sugar, please refer back to page 18.

Again, I prefer making this buttercream fresh every time I want to use it, but bringing it back from the refrigerator is a little bit more forgiving. I have yet to split this buttercream, but it is important to leave it to soften before mixing it or using it again.

French buttercream recipe

This makes enough to fill, stack and decorate a 15cm/6in
cake. It can be made in a standard-sized stand mixer.

YOU WILL NEED
small/medium saucepan
stand mixer with whisk attachment
sugar thermometer
pastry brush with a cupful of water

INGREDIENTS
360g/12½oz/scant 2 cups caster sugar
75ml/2½fl oz/5 tbsp cold or tepid tap water
180g/6¼oz egg yolks
500g/1lb 2oz/scant 2¼ cups unsalted butter at room temperature, cut into cubes

1 In a small/medium saucepan, combine the sugar
and water and stir with the tip of your finger to make
sure there is no sugar sticking on the bottom of the pan.

2 In the stand mixer bowl, add the egg yolks and
attach the whisk attachment.

3 Start heating up the sugar and water over a
medium heat, with a sugar thermometer and a pastry
brush and water at the ready.

*If any sugar crystals come up the side, wash them
down using the pastry brush.*

4 Start whisking the egg yolks on a high speed to get
them thick and fluffy.

5 Once the sugar starts bubbling, start taking the
temperature. When the sugar reaches 'soft ball' stage
(116–120°C/241–248°F), carefully take the saucepan
off the heat.

*At this point, the egg yolks should be pale and doubled
in volume.*

6 Lower the speed of the mixer to medium and very
carefully pour the sugar down the side of the bowl
into the whisking egg yolks, trying to avoid hitting the
whisk with the sugar.

7 Once all the sugar is inside, increase the speed of
the mixer again and continue whisking for 5 minutes.
After 5 minutes, the bowl should have cooled down.
If it hasn't, then either continue whisking or turn the
mixer off and leave it to cool.

*If you add the butter in too early, the butter will melt
rather than form the buttercream!*

8 Now it's time to add the butter, just like how we did
with the Swiss meringue buttercream. On a medium
speed, slowly add the butter, one cube at a time.

*This buttercream comes together much quicker than
Swiss meringue buttercream.*

9 Once all the butter is added and the buttercream
has thickened up, speed up the mixer to fully
incorporate all the ingredients.

10 Turn off the mixer and your buttercream is ready
to flavour!

*This buttercream can be flavoured in the same way as
Swiss meringue buttercream. See previous recipes on
pages 55–56 for buttercream flavourings.*

Chocolate ganache

This lesson is just touching the surface of the world of ganache. Chocolate ganache is a combination of cream and chocolate. Once cooled, it becomes a luxurious, spreadable consistency, which has the richest taste of chocolate without being too heavy. I use chocolate ganache as my chocolate drips on a cake (which we will visit again later in the book), but it also makes a delicious cake filling as well as a macaron filling, too.

You can make ganache from any percentage of chocolate and the process remains the same; however, the ratio of cream will differ depending on what chocolate you are using and for what purpose.

Cream acts as the fat in this recipe, so the darker the chocolate, the less the fat content in the chocolate and therefore more cream needs to be used. The lighter the chocolate (especially white chocolate) the higher the fat content and so less cream is added to make ganache. Cream also differs in fat content. I like using a double cream or a high-fat cream for my ganache (usually between 38 and 42% fat).

Note: *for all my recipes that use chocolate, I use couverture chocolate chips, but if you are using a bar of chocolate instead, roughly chop the chocolate into small pieces before use.*

Ganache recipes to fill and stack a 15cm/6in cake

See page 118 for ganache drip recipes.

Whipping cream (36–38% fat)

SEMI-DARK CHOCOLATE (54%):
1:2 (260ml/9¼fl oz/generous 1 cup cream, 520g/1lb 3oz choc)

MILK CHOCOLATE (33%):
1:3 (200ml/7fl oz/scant 1 cup cream, 600g/1lb 5oz choc)

WHITE CHOCOLATE (28%):
1:4 (160ml/5¼fl oz/⅔ cup cream, 640g/1lb 6½oz choc)

Double cream (42–48% fat)

SEMI-DARK CHOCOLATE (54%):
1:1 (400ml/14fl oz/1¾ cups cream, 400g/14oz choc)

MILK CHOCOLATE (33%):
1:2 (260ml/9¼fl oz/generous 1 cup cream, 520g/1lb 3oz choc)

WHITE CHOCOLATE (28%):
1:3 (200ml/7fl oz/scant 1 cup cream, 600g/1lb 5oz choc)

Saucepan method

Whenever I work with chocolate and need to heat it, I like using a
saucepan rather than a microwave because I can control exactly what is
going on in front of me. Chocolate can overheat quite easily and there
is no way of bringing it back, so you have to keep an eye on it at all times!

YOU WILL NEED
small saucepan
heatproof bowl
whisk
clingfilm

1 Add the cream to a small saucepan and place it over a medium heat.

2 Place the chocolate in a heatproof bowl.

3 Once the cream is steaming (not boiling!), remove the pan from the heat.

4 Pour the chocolate into the saucepan on top of the cream and stir it using a whisk.

The whisk helps incorporate the ingredients quicker than a spatula does.

5 Once the chocolate and cream have completely combined, transfer it back into the bowl.

6 Once cooled, cover the bowl with clingfilm or transfer the ganache into an airtight container and leave the ganache to set for 5–12 hours at room temperature.

7 The ganache is ready when it's a thick yet spreadable consistency.

Microwave method

I'll be honest, microwaving chocolate scares me because it can burn or seize so easily; however, using the microwave is definitely the easiest and quickest method! If you are using a microwave, be sure to melt the chocolate in short 20–30-second bursts. As I mentioned earlier, I usually do this on high/full power, but microwave ovens vary, so adjust the setting used to suit your model. Remember, when working with chocolate, it's always better to err on the safe side.

YOU WILL NEED
heatproof bowl
clingfilm (optional)

1 Place the cream and chocolate into a heatproof bowl.

2 Melt together in the microwave in 20–30-second bursts, stirring in between each burst.

Note: *the ratios with more chocolate will take longer to melt than the ratios with more cream.*

3 Once melted, stir it to make sure there are no more lumps of chocolate left.

4 Leave to cool completely.

5 Transfer into an airtight container or cover the bowl with clingfilm and leave the ganache to set for 5–12 hours at room temperature.

6 The ganache is ready when it's a thick yet spreadable consistency.

Things to note

• The time that the ganache takes to set is determined by the room temperature. In the winter months, ganache can set in a couple of hours, whereas in the summer, it's best to leave it overnight.

• If your ganache splits, add some more cream and stir it in. You can also use a stick blender to held bind the ganache together again.

• Using cheaper/bad quality chocolate can result in split ganache. These recipes are based on using couverture chocolate chips (see page 20 for an explanation on this).

Reheating ganache

Unlike buttercream, ganache is very easy to reheat, which means you can also make it ahead of time and keep it in the refrigerator until you need it. Hopefully, once having left ganache to set over a few hours, it will be at perfect consistency to work with. Occasionally, ganache hardens a little too much and it requires loosening up a bit.

TO REHEAT GANACHE, IT'S QUITE SIMPLE AND THERE ARE A COUPLE OF WAYS IN WHICH YOU CAN DO SO:

1 Half-fill a saucepan with water and heat until it's simmering. Place the bowl of ganache over the top of the water and leave it until you start to see the ganache starting to melt. Mix the ganache with a rubber spatula to try and maintain the distribution of heat in the bowl. Continue heating until it becomes the correct consistency.

2 In a microwave, heat up the bowl of ganache in 10-second bursts (see page 65). Wait until it's soft enough to start mixing with a rubber spatula, then continue heating in short bursts until it becomes the correct consistency.

Working with ganache feels very different to buttercream when applying it to a cake; however, the techniques are the same. Throughout the cake decorating section of this book, I will focus on buttercream applications, but you can use the same techniques to apply ganache. Ganache is all about keeping it at the correct consistency at all times, so you may need a pan of hot water on the go at the same time as working with it (especially in the winter!).

Things to note

• If the ganache gets too soft, take it off the heat and mix it thoroughly, then leave it to set until it becomes the desired consistency.

• Once ganache has set the first time around, it takes less time to set again.

• There is a chance that the ganache can split when reheating. If this happens, blend the loose ganache with a stick blender to bind the fat and chocolate together again.

• Once made, ganache will keep in an airtight container in the refrigerator for up to 1 month. I usually keep it in a metal bowl covered with clingfilm, then reheat it gently in the bowl placed over a pan of gently simmering water to bring it back to the correct consistency (use a microwave-safe bowl if reheating it in a microwave).

Jam

Jam and cream is the most classic combination of flavours when it comes to cakes, at least in the UK. The balance of tart fruit and the sweetness of the buttercream is a real match made in heaven. The best part about jam is that it's readily available and you can easily purchase a jar of pretty much any flavour. You can use it for a cake and have leftovers for your toast, too! If you feel a little bit adventurous, or if you have some berries that are on their last day and you don't want them to go to waste, making a jam is a great way to use them up and makes an excellent filling for your cakes.

Referring back to the sugar temperatures that I explained on page 18, the first stage of the sugar heating process is the 'thread' stage. Thread refers to the temperature of the sugar and fruit when making jam. In fact, some traditional sugar thermometers may even have 'jam' written on them next to this temperature range.

To make a basic jam, the recipe is extremely simple. It's equal amounts of sugar and fruit, plus some lemon juice. I find that berry jams work best in cakes because they tend to be more sour and the jam won't be too sweet. I've included an example recipe over the page using raspberries (which is my favourite) but you can pretty much use any berries. Larger fruits contain more water and therefore the quantities of sugar can differ.

Raspberry jam

Makes a medium jam jarful (about 380g/13oz)

YOU WILL NEED
sterilized medium jam jar
saucepan
heatproof rubber spatula or wooden spoon
sugar thermometer

INGREDIENTS
300g/10½oz raspberries (fresh or frozen)
300g/10½oz/1½ cups caster sugar
juice of one lemon

1 Begin by sterilizing a clean jam jar. Do this by either submerging the jar and lid in boiling water in a pan for 10 minutes, or placing the jar in a preheated oven at 180°C/160°C fan/gas 4 for 10 minutes and boiling only the lid in a pan of hot water for the same length of time.

2 In a saucepan, combine the berries and sugar and set the heat to medium. With a rubber spatula or wooden spoon, crush the berries and continue to stir. Eventually the water will release from the fruit and the sugar will begin to melt.

3 Continue to stir until the fruit starts to bubble. Start to read the temperature with the sugar thermometer, stirring every minute or so.

Because the sugar is mixed with the fruit, it's okay to stir the sugar!

4 When the jam reaches 107°C/225°F ('thread' stage), take it off the heat and leave for 5–10 minutes.

5 Add in the lemon juice and mix through.

The lemon juice will loosen up the jam as it will have thickened over the heat and when cooling down.

6 Carefully pour the jam into the sterilized jar and seal the jar lid shut, then leave to cool completely.

Once made, and presuming the jar is 100% sterile, the jam will last for months! As long as the ratio of fruit to sugar remains the same, you can get creative with flavours such as mixing berries or adding lemon or lime zest for extra zing!

Store the jam in a cool, dry place away from direct sunlight for up to 12 months. Once opened, store the jam in the refrigerator and use within 1 month.

Curd

We've covered which filling to make with berries, now let's visit the citrus fruits. Citrus is known for its sour notes and, naturally, we relate it to summery vibrant flavours. Whether it's lemon, lime or orange, making a curd and sandwiching it in-between layers of buttercream really makes a cake sing with flavour. Similar to jam, as long as the ratio of fruit juice is kept the same, you can get creative in the curd flavours you make. I have made everything from lime to passion fruit curd, but here is the recipe for a classic lemon curd with the perfect level of sweetness and tartness.

This recipe works with both whole eggs and egg yolks. Because I use so many egg whites in my buttercream recipe, I like any excuse to use up my egg yolks. I find the texture of the lemon curd is slightly thicker than when using whole eggs, too, which some people prefer.

Lemon curd

Makes about 450g/1lb

YOU WILL NEED
small saucepan
two heatproof bowls
heatproof rubber spatula
sieve
clingfilm

INGREDIENTS
finely grated zest and juice of 3 lemons
150g/5½oz/¾ cup caster sugar
150g/5½oz eggs or egg yolks
30g/1oz/2 tbsp unsalted butter, cut into cubes

1 Fill a small saucepan with about 5cm/2in of water and place over a low heat until simmering.

2 In a heatproof bowl, combine the lemon zest and juice and the sugar and mix using a rubber spatula until all of the sugar has released from the bottom of the bowl.

3 Keep the water over a low heat and place the bowl over the saucepan.

4 In a separate small bowl, break up the eggs/yolks using a fork.

5 Continue stirring the juice and sugar until you can feel that the sugar has dissolved into the juice.

6 Pour the eggs/yolks into the bowl and mix using a spatula until the eggs are fully combined.

7 Continue stirring for about 5 minutes until the mixture has thickened up, enough to hold itself.

8 Remove the bowl from the saucepan and pass the curd through a sieve into a clean heatproof bowl.

The sieve should catch the lemon zest and any egg lumps that may not have mixed in properly.

9 While the curd is still hot, add in the butter and mix with a rubber spatula (use the one from earlier, just give it a quick rinse first) until the butter has melted and combined.

10 Cover the bowl with clingfilm and press the clingfilm down so it's touching the surface of the curd in the bowl – this prevents a skin from forming or any condensation dripping down onto the curd.

11 Leave to cool completely before using (if storing for later use, carefully pour the hot lemon curd into a sterilized jar instead and seal the jar lid shut, then leave to cool completely).

Stored in a sterilized jar, lemon curd will keep for up to 2 weeks in the refrigerator. See my previous jam recipe on page 70 to see how you can sterilize a jar suitable for keeping your spreads fresh! For this recipe, I would use a large jam jar or Mason (Kilner-type) jar. However, if I'm using the curd within the next couple of days, then I prefer to simply store it in a bowl covered with clingfilm in the refrigerator.

Salted caramel

I'm not sure when the fashion of salted caramel started, but I'm so thankful that it did. In fact, when I taste caramel without added salt, I feel like it's missing something! Caramel's main ingredient is, of course, sugar, and therefore a caramel sauce is probably one of the sweetest fillings. Adding salt cuts the sweetness and also enhances the caramel flavour. No wonder it took over the dessert world! I briefly mentioned caramel earlier when I explained the heating process of sugar, but this caramel isn't just made from sugar. With the addition of butter and cream, it allows the caramel to become more of a sauce rather than a brittle piece of cooked sugar.

This caramel sauce is so versatile. It can be used to fill chocolates, macarons and cakes, as well as being added to buttercream to flavour, and it's even used for dripping down the sides of a cake, too! Once again, sterilizing a jar (see page 70) before making this sauce means that you can keep it for longer (if you don't eat it beforehand that is!).

Makes a medium jarful (about 400g/14oz)

YOU WILL NEED
large saucepan
heatproof rubber spatula
sieve
heatproof bowl or sterilized jar
clingfilm

INGREDIENTS
200g/7oz/1 cup caster or granulated sugar
1 tsp salt
90g/3¼oz/generous ⅓ cup unsalted butter, at room temperature, cut into cubes
120ml/4fl oz/½ cup double cream or 100ml/3½fl oz/scant ½ cup whipping cream, at room temperature

Top Tip

Caramel sauce can be kept in an airtight container for 2–3 days at room temperature (it will retain a more loose consistency at room temperature), or it can be stored in an airtight container or sealed jar in the refrigerator for up to 2 weeks. Caramel sauce will thicken up once it's cooled and refrigerated. It can be used straight from the refrigerator (depending on the consistency required), and it can also be easily reheated in a bain-marie or in short bursts in the microwave if a runnier consistency is required (Note: the caramel can get very hot, so be careful when reheating it).

1 In a large saucepan, sprinkle the sugar so it's a thin layer on the bottom of the pan. Put the saucepan over a medium heat and add the salt.

2 Every 30 seconds, gently shake the pan to move the sugar around.

3 When the sugar starts to stick to the bottom of the pan, you can shake it a bit more vigorously.

You don't want to stir the sugar at this point as it may interfere with the caramelizing of the sugar granules and cause it to crystallize.

4 If there are areas of the sugar that start to caramelize before other areas start to melt, use a rubber spatula to slowly move the sugar around the pan.

5 Continue moving the sugar around the pan until all the sugar has completely dissolved and it's a rich amber colour.

6 Add the butter and quickly stir until it's completely melted into the sugar.

The caramel will bubble vigorously at this point – it's very hot so be careful!

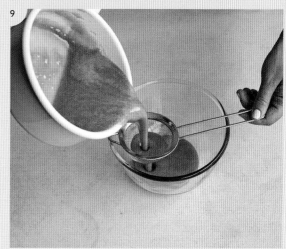

7 Slowly pour in the cream, stirring at the same time, and continue stirring until the cream has fully mixed in.

If the cream is too cold, it can cause the caramel to seize and become clumpy.

8 Leave the caramel to bubble for about 20 seconds and then remove the pan from the heat.

You can skip this bubbling part if the caramel is dark in colour already.

9 Pass the caramel through a sieve into a heatproof bowl or a sterilized jar.

I like to pass the caramel through a sieve to make sure there are no clumps of sugar and the sauce is completely smooth.

10 Cover and seal the jar lid shut or cover the bowl with clingfilm, allowing the clingfilm to touch the surface of the caramel to prevent it forming a skin – but don't touch the caramel! It is very hot!

11 Leave to cool completely before handling or using.

CAKE BUILDING

So, our sponge cakes, buttercream and fillings are prepared, now it's time to start building up a layered cake. Cutting, layering and stacking a cake is usually the more messy part of the cake decoration process, so keeping clean and organized is key! Make sure you have everything you need in preparation for this process and give yourself plenty of time. After all, nobody likes working under time pressure.

Torting cakes

Torting a cake is a fancy way of saying 'cutting the cake horizontally into thinner layers'. I've previously mentioned that cakes have become taller over the years, which means there are more layers of cake and buttercream than there used to be (which can only be a good thing, right?!). The reason why I like baking my cakes in two tins is that I know I can then divide each cake in half and have a total of four layers. Some people prefer baking their cakes in multiple tins to avoid the torting process. While torting cakes can seem nerve-racking, you actually end up wasting less cake and here's why.

When a cake is baked in a tin, the bottom of the cake touches the base of the tin and the top part will have risen and usually forms a slight dome. That bottom edge of the cake will be the straightest edge and so I like to take advantage of its shape and use it as the bottom or top layer of cake. The top domed part of the cake will need evening out so if there are more tins to level, more cake will be cut away.

There is another reason why I only like to use two tins for one cake. When a cake is baked, there is a darker layer of crumb around the outside of the sponge and the inside is much lighter (apart from chocolate cake which is dark both around the edges and in the centre). When the domed edge is trimmed, we are also getting rid of that thin layer of crumb on the top, leaving the crumb layer around the edges and base of the cake. Let's refer to this crumb layer as the outline of the cake.

My pet hate is when you have a beautiful pale yellow sponge cake, filled with glorious white buttercream and then as you cut into the cake a dark brown crumb layer is revealed right in the centre, breaking up the delicate whiteness of the cake. If the crumb outline is only around the edge of the cake, it looks much neater and overall looks better quality. If you bake the cake in several tins, each layer will have this crumb edge (unless you trim it off which wastes even more cake). And you won't have this outline around the outer edge of the cake.

So now I've convinced you to bake your cakes in two tins, let's get torting.

REMOVING THE DOMED PART OF THE CAKE

1 Place your bread knife at the very top of the cake, just above the corner of the cake where the dome on top starts.

2 Rather than moving the knife, start rotating the cake towards the knife and drag the knife around the top edge of the cake marking a line.

3 You now have a guide showing where to cut. If the line has moved up or down, retrace where you've cut until the knife meets where you started.

4 Once you have a levelled line around the cake, you can start cutting into the cake.

5 Continue turning the cake and begin sawing the knife gradually.

6 Keep turning the cake as you cut and eventually the knife goes through the middle of the cake and the top part comes off.

REPEAT ON THE SECOND CAKE

7 Now you have one cake trimmed, you can use it as a guide for your next one.

8 Place the second cake next to the first and rest your bread knife on top of the ready-cut cake.

9 Keep the knife in the same place as you turn the second cake (as it should remain straight) and repeat the same process.

10 Having the guide from the first cake will ensure that both of your cakes remain at the same height.

CUTTING THE CAKE IN HALF TO GET TWO LAYERS OF CAKE

11 Bend down so you can see where halfway up the cake is.

12 Place your bread knife halfway up the side of the cake and without cutting in, trace a line around the outside of the cake by turning the sponge, just like before.

13 If you move the knife and the line isn't straight, retrace the line until you meet back where you started.

14 Once you have a straight line around the cake, start to cut with the knife, continuously rotating the cake at the same time.

15 Continue cutting and turning until the knife goes through the middle of the cake and the top layer comes away. You should now have two flat layers of cake.

18

REPEAT ON THE SECOND CAKE

16 Rest your bread knife on one of the halves of the first cake and bring the uncut cake next to it.

17 Use the height of the cut layer to trace the knife around the sides of the cake.

18 Once you have the guide, you can start cutting and repeat the same process as before to get another two flat layers of cake, making a total of four flat layers of cake.

19 At this point, I like to soak my cake layers with my Sugar Soaking Syrup (see page 44). I apply the syrup over each cake layer using a pastry brush or a soaking syrup bottle (see page 46) until the surface of each layer is lightly moistened by the syrup. This allows these layers of cake to soak up some of the syrup (as well as getting this messy part out of the way!).

18

PREPARE YOUR CAKES IN ORDER OF STACKING

20 Now we have four layers of cake in total: two with a crumb surface and two without. What I like to do here is stack the layers in the same order that I want to stack them when building up my cake. This is purely for organization – as I mentioned earlier, being organized is key. The two surfaces of the cake that were touching the cake tin are completely flat so I like to use one as the bottom layer and one as the top layer upside down. Not only does this keep the crumb layer on the outer edges of the cake, it also ensures that the base and top of the cake are perfectly flat, which will help me achieve a straight and even cake when I'm decorating it with buttercream.

20

Layering

Cake makers have their own methods for layering up a cake with buttercream and fillings. Having made cakes for several years myself, as well as teaching people how to decorate cakes, I've developed specific techniques which I believe to be the most efficient way to achieve a tall and straight cake. From knowing the amount of filling between each layer to holding the palette knife in the correct position, follow my step-by-step guidance and you'll have yourself a perfectly stacked cake.

So before we get layering, let's fill up a piping bag with buttercream. I prefer using a piping bag when building up a cake with buttercream because it keeps things clean and it helps achieve an even layer of buttercream more efficiently than applying it with a palette knife. I used to just spoon on some buttercream and spread it out with a palette knife, but the layers between the cakes weren't even because I never knew how much buttercream I was putting on at one time. There's nothing better than slicing into a cake and revealing those perfectly even layers.

Piping is a skill that needs practice so it may feel a bit strange at first, but trust me, after practising multiple times, it will become second nature and you won't think twice about it. The best way to fill a piping bag is as follows:

1 Take a tall glass, large enough to fit most of your piping bag in.

2 Place the piping bag in the glass so the point is facing down and the wider open part is coming out of the top of the glass.

3 Fold down the edges of the piping bag around the outside of the glass (this prevents this part of the bag from getting dirty).

4 Using a spoon or spatula, fill up the piping bag with your buttercream.

5 Lift the piping bag up from the glass and twist the top of the piping bag shut – the piping bag shouldn't be more than two-thirds full.

6 Cut off the pointed end of the piping bag about 2cm/¾in from the bottom, and now you can push the buttercream through the piping bag.

Note: *we don't need a piping nozzle/tip to fill up the cake with buttercream, that comes later!*

Layering the cake with buttercream

The buttercream is now prepared in a piping bag, the cakes
are cut and ready, now let's focus on the equipment needed: a
turntable with a non-slip piece of material or a wet piece of kitchen
paper underneath so the cake doesn't move around, a cake
board, a step palette knife, a side scraper and a spare bowl.
Now we're ready to layer.

1 Place the cake board on the turntable.

2 Before we start filling the cake, we need to secure
the cake to our cake board. Squeeze a small amount
of buttercream onto the centre of the cake board
by applying pressure to the top of the piping bag
and letting the buttercream come out of the open
end (keep the bag twisted at the top to avoid any
buttercream spilling out!).

3 Take your first cake layer (one of the layers with the
crumb base) and place it onto the cake board, so the
crumb layer is facing downwards. Give it a good push
downwards so it's securely stuck to the buttercream.

4 Now apply a layer of buttercream on top of the
surface of the cake. I find it easiest to start in the

Photo Steps Continue Overleaf _____

centre and squeeze a spiral of buttercream all the way out towards the edges of the cake. Try to keep the pressure even while piping the spiral to allow the same amount of buttercream to come out all the way across this layer of cake. This will make it easier to maintain an even layer of buttercream.

5 Now we're going to flatten out this layer of buttercream even more. Hold the step palette knife, firmly in your hand and place it gently on the surface of the buttercream with the bent part of the palette knife in the centre of the cake. Slightly tilt the knife away from you so only one edge of it is touching the surface of the buttercream and you can see underneath the blade. Start turning the turntable towards the palette knife (for example, if you're holding your palette knife in your right hand, turn the turntable clockwise). Gently apply pressure on the blade of the palette knife as you turn the cake. The straight edge of the palette knife should flatten out the buttercream even more as well as eradicate air bubbles, creating a smooth, even surface. If you put too much pressure towards the edges of the palette knife, you'll end up with a cone-shaped mound of buttercream. To avoid this, focus the pressure in the centre of the cake as you rotate the turntable. If there is a slight mound in the middle of the cake, you can go over it with one swipe using the same edge of the palette knife. The next cake layer will be going on top of this so it doesn't have to be 100% perfect, but the straighter this layer is, the straighter the cake will be. Once you are happy with this layer of buttercream, you can move onto the next step.

6 Take one of the centre layers of cake and place it onto this layer of buttercream. Try and make sure it's as lined up as possible to avoid touching it more later on. I find it easier to pipe on the flattest side – i.e. the edge that was cut from the centre of the (domed) cake.

7 Repeat the same process as before with piping a layer of buttercream onto the surface of this cake layer. Once again, flatten out with the palette knife until you achieve a smooth even layer of buttercream.

8 Take the remaining centre layer of cake and place it on top of the second layer of buttercream. Again, line the cake layer up with the other layers that are already sandwiched with buttercream and repeat the same process, piping on another even layer of buttercream and flattening it out with the palette knife. Don't worry if any buttercream is overspilling on the outside of the cake.

9 Finally, place on the remaining cake layer, only this time, turn it upside down so the crumb layer is facing upwards. As mentioned previously, this is the flattest part of the cake so we want to take advantage of its shape! Now is also the time to make sure that all of your cake layers are in line with each other so if you need to, you can adjust them now.

Layering the cake with buttercream and an added filling

In the previous chapter, we covered some delicious recipes for fillings that you can add to your cake. Fillings such as jam and curd are much looser than buttercream and can therefore spill out of the edges of the cake and can even cause it to slide. If you want to add a filling, an extra step has to be taken when layering your cake.

When piping the layer of buttercream, rather than starting from the inside and piping a spiral to the outside edge of the cake, you need to create something called a dam. This is where a ring of buttercream is piped around the outside edge of the cake to act as a barrier for the filling. Then the filling is added to the middle followed by a layer of buttercream on top. This method not only prevents the cake from sliding around, it also ensures that every slice of cake has the same ratio of sponge, buttercream and filling.

1 Similar to the previous process, first place the cake board on the turntable, then secure the cake to the cake board with a little bit of buttercream.

2 Next, place the first layer of cake onto the cake board and press it down to secure it (make sure the crumb layer is facing downwards).

3 Pipe a ring of buttercream around the outside edge of the cake, trying to keep the thickness the same all the way around.

4 Using a teaspoon, add some of your chosen filling to the centre of cake and spread it out flat, keeping it inside this ring of buttercream.

Don't add too much filling at this point as it can cause the cake to slide – remember there are four layers of this cake so there will be plenty of filling inside!

5 Now pipe the buttercream on top of this filling so the whole surface is completely covered in buttercream.

6 Just like before, use the side of your palette knife and flatten out this layer of buttercream.

7 Continue the stacking process in the same way as before, adding your filling in between the buttercream layers each time.

Layering the cake with a piñata filling

A celebration cake is all about that WOW factor. Something that became a huge cake trend in recent years is a piñata cake. This is when you slice a cake and as you take the piece away there's a surprise of either sprinkles, chocolate or sweets that comes spilling out from the middle. A piñata filling is a fun way to reveal a gender at a baby shower, to enhance a theme at a birthday party or even just to add that theatrical moment to your showstopper.

1 Before you layer your cake, you will need to prepare your sponge cake layers. Take a small round biscuit/ cookie cutter (about 4cm/1½in in diameter for a 15cm/6in cake) and use it to cut a hole out of the centre of all the cake layers. (You can use a slightly larger cutter for larger cakes, if you like, but bear in mind that more sprinkles/filling will make more of a mess when cutting!)

2 Take the two pieces that were taken from the crumb layer and cut them in half horizontally to make them thinner (you can discard – or eat! – the remaining pieces).

Photo Steps Continue Overleaf _____

3 Place the cake board on the turntable, then secure the first layer of cake (with the crumb edge facing downwards) onto the board with some buttercream and place one of the thinner circles of cake (see step 2) back into the centre of the layer. It should be half the height of the rest of the cake layer.

4 Start layering your cake with buttercream, just like before, only this time, pipe it around the centre hole and try not to let any buttercream fall into the centre.

5 Even out the buttercream with your palette knife.

6 Continue building up your cake layers with layers of buttercream. If there is an overspill of buttercream in the centre where the hole is, you can clean it away with your palette knife by wiping it around the hole in the centre.

7 For the last cake layer, flip the cake upside down so the crumb edge is facing upwards.

8 Now is the time to fill your centre with your chosen filling! I prefer smaller chocolates/sweets than sprinkles, purely because I think they're nicer to eat

6

7

8

9

and don't make as much mess when cutting the cake! Choose your filling with the purpose of the cake in mind. For example, if it's a rainbow cake, use multicoloured sweets, if it's a baby shower, use your chosen colour, etc.

9 Once the filling has reached just below the top of the cake, take the remaining thinner circle that was cut out earlier (see step 2) and place it upside down on the top of the cake to close and secure the hole. Now the filling is sealed in the cake.

Note: *certain fillings such as sugar-coated chocolate may soften over time. If you need to keep your cake for a few days, choose a harder filling such as sweets or sprinkles.*

Crumb coat

What is a crumb coat? A crumb coat is a thin layer of buttercream that is applied around the whole cake to encase the crumbs inside. Once the crumb coat has been applied, the cake sets in the refrigerator or freezer until the layer of buttercream is completely hard. This prevents any loose crumbs getting inside the second clean layer of buttercream that will coat the cake. Any cake, whether it's round, square or shaped, needs a crumb coat.

Note the words 'thin layer'. During the crumb coat process, buttercream will get contaminated with crumbs. It's important to try not to make too much of your buttercream 'dirty' with crumbs because it will essentially go to waste. I always try to use as little buttercream as possible for the crumb coat so I have as much buttercream as possible for the decorating part.

1   To begin the crumb coat, we need to add a small amount of buttercream to the outside of the cake. I like piping between the layers of cake where there is buttercream already. Some of the buttercream is already overspilling, but sometimes there are larger gaps. Pipe between these layers to pack out that buttercream which also prevents any air pockets inside the cake, too.

2   Pipe a small amount of buttercream on top of the cake and start spreading that out with your palette knife. Spread the buttercream using the outer edges of the palette knife, moving it side to side while turning your turntable to spread it out evenly towards the outer edges of the cake.

3   Repeat the same smoothing out motion when filling up a cake. Place the bent part of the palette knife in the centre of the cake, tilt the palette knife slightly and turn the turntable to achieve a smooth flat finish of buttercream on the top of the cake. The buttercream starts to push out towards the edges of the cake – this is a good thing as it will help us achieve sharp defined corners later on.

4   Now let's focus on spreading out the buttercream around the sides of the cake. Every time you are spreading buttercream on the side of a cake, the palette knife has to be straight at all times. Introducing 'the cake stance': this is where we work on the opposite

Photo Steps Continue Overleaf _____

side of the cake to the hand that you're holding the palette knife in while holding the palette knife upside down. For me, I hold my palette knife in my right hand, but I work on the left hand side of the cake. This ensures that the blade of the palette knife is constantly straight against the sides of the cake – there is no other angle that the palette knife is straight. It may feel strange at first but you get used to it very quickly!

5 Keeping in this position, move the palette knife side to side, again using the outer edges of the blade to spread the buttercream around the outside of the cake. Use the turntable to help you move the buttercream, starting from the bottom of the cake and working towards the top. Don't worry about smoothing out the buttercream at this point as this will come in the next step.

6 Once the whole cake has a thin layer of buttercream over the top and sides, it's time to scrape. When holding the side scraper, make sure your fingers are spread out, your hand is towards the bottom and you're placing the scraper against the cake at a 45° angle towards you. The best way to keep your scraper straight is to imagine that you are cleaning the bottom of the cake board with the bottom of the scraper. Once you have the scraper in position you can start turning the turntable towards the scraper, keeping it in the same position at all times and avoiding the cake from touching the wide surface of the scraper, only the very edge. Don't push against the cake with too much pressure as you will be at risk of tearing the cake. Go around the cake multiple times and you will start re-distributing the buttercream around the cake, filling in any pockets where there isn't enough buttercream and taking off excess where there is too much.

7 Once you've gone around the cake multiple times and have a significant build-up of buttercream on your scraper, you can remove the excess buttercream using your palette knife and place it into a separate bowl – not into the bowl where your clean buttercream is! You can use this crumby buttercream to fill in any gaps or air pockets where there isn't enough buttercream on the cake. Once again, if you are using your palette knife, make sure you are holding it in the same position as in step 4.

8 Continue scraping the buttercream around the cake until you achieve an even layer of buttercream around the sides of the cake.

To avoid getting lines down the cake where you have come on or off with the scraper, begin turning the turntable slightly before you place the scraper on the cake so it glides on without creating a line. When coming off with the scraper, come off with a sweeping movement rather than stopping and lifting off, as this causes lines in the buttercream.

9 When most of the buttercream is smooth, I like to go around the cake with one long movement with the scraper. With my scraper in my right hand, I bring my left hand to the back of the turntable and bring the turntable all the way around until my arms cross over, keeping the scraper in the same position at all times. I find that this technique is what gives the buttercream a smooth and overall finish.

10 You may have noticed that working around the sides of the cake causes the buttercream to come upwards around the top corners, so now it's time to clean them off. Note that this is the last step to do, once you clean the corners you cannot touch the sides of the cake again otherwise it pushes buttercream back upwards. With the outer edge of the palette knife, travel from the outside of the cake into the centre just skimming over the top edge where there is an excess of buttercream. Once your palette knife comes to the centre of the cake, lift it off – be careful not to swipe it over to the other side because you will knock the buttercream off in the wrong direction and have to work on the sides again! Clean your palette knife from buttercream by wiping it on your scraper or the edge of the bowl and repeat the whole way around the cake, bringing the buttercream inwards all the way around the cake.

11 Chill your cake in the refrigerator for 30 minutes or in the freezer for 15 minutes until this layer of buttercream has completely firmed up.

Note: *This is a crumb coat and not the finished look of the cake so it doesn't have to be perfect! What you're aiming to achieve is for the shape of the cake to be as straight as possible. If there are air bubbles or the buttercream isn't perfectly smooth, this can be corrected in the next stage!*

A shortcut to layering

This method is definitely a shortcut to layering up your cake and making it as straight as possible at the same time. I find this process to be the most helpful, especially when I want to add a filling, as it's the most effective way to keep it inside the layers of cake without it seeping out. This process does involve an extra step in the refrigerator or freezer than the other method; however, it still cuts time significantly and your cake always comes out beautifully straight!

1 Take one of the tins that you baked your cakes in (round 15cm/6in in diameter and at least 7.5cm/3in deep) and line the inside edges with a thin sheet of acetate – it should come up higher than the tin.

If you don't have access to acetate, this also works by doubling up some baking paper.

2 Put a small piece of baking paper at the bottom of the tin and place the first layer of cake inside the tin with the crumb layer facing downwards.

3 Pipe a ring of buttercream around the outer edge of this layer of cake, making sure the buttercream is touching the acetate/baking paper.

4 If you want to add a filling, add this now and spread it out evenly (the angle is slightly awkward here, I find using a small spoon is the best way to spread it out).

5 If you've added a filling, pipe the buttercream on top so the whole surface is covered in buttercream. If no filling has been added, pipe a layer of buttercream on the cake directly.

6 Place on the second (centre) layer of cake and press it down, ensuring that it's level.

Note that we didn't level out the buttercream with the palette knife – because of the acetate we're able to press the second cake layer down hard enough to flatten out the buttercream underneath.

7 Repeat the same process as before, piping a ring of buttercream around the outside of the cake, then adding your chosen filling inside.

8 Continue until the last piece of cake is added at the top, upside down so the crumb layer is facing upwards (make sure it's completely level – use the edge of the acetate as a guide).

9 Place the whole tin in the refrigerator for 30 minutes or in the freezer for 15 minutes until the buttercream is set.

Now to finish the crumb coat.

Photo Steps Continue Overleaf _____

10 When needed, remove the cake from the refrigerator or freezer and, using scissors, trim the acetate to the height of the cake.

11 Place the cake board on the turntable. Pipe some buttercream on your cake board.

12 Flip the cake upside down onto the cake board, centre and secure it to the buttercream.

13 Carefully lift up the tin and remove the acetate or baking paper from the outside of the cake.

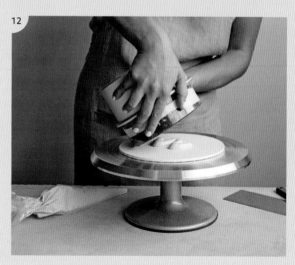

13

13

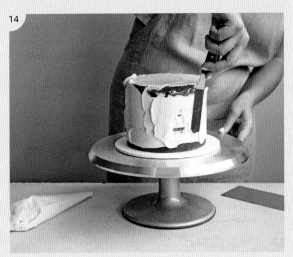

14

14 Continue as for applying a regular crumb coat (see page 99). There won't be significant gaps in between the layers because the buttercream was pressed against the acetate/baking paper, so pipe a small amount on top of what's already there.

15 Finish the crumb coat and chill your cake in the refrigerator for 30 minutes or in the freezer for 15 minutes until the buttercream has completely firmed up.

Your crumb-coated cake is now setting in the refrigerator or freezer, which means we are finished with crumbs! This is the perfect opportunity to reset your workspace. Wipe away any crumbs left on the surface, clean your equipment and discard or put away any leftover buttercream that's contaminated with crumbs.

Once the cake has a crumb coat, the sponge is airtight with buttercream and can stay fresh. If I am ever decorating multiple cakes at once, I finish all of the crumb coats, then completely clean down my kitchen and even make new buttercream for my second coating. Sometimes, I spread the decorating over two days: day one, crumb coats; day two, second buttercream layer. Not only does this keep the whole cake decorating process a lot more relaxed and organized, but you are guaranteed a crumb-free zone the next day. We don't want any cake crumbs in our clean buttercream for the second layer on the cake, which is coming next.

COVERING
WITH
BUTTERCREAM

This is the decorating stage. The tips and techniques you will learn in this chapter will apply to any cake that you decorate. The application of buttercream may differ, but essentially, you are aiming for a smooth, even layer of buttercream to coat your cake.

Colouring buttercream

Even though this may not sound like an important stage, colouring is what gives your cake a theme and purpose. Colouring itself is like an art and it's important not only to know which colours go well together but also how to adapt the colours depending on what design you're making and, of course, which kind of food colouring to use.

Let's just rule out one kind of food colouring from the start. LIQUIDS. Never use liquid food colouring. Liquid food colouring is weak in colour, therefore you need a large quantity to achieve any sort of shade, which then dramatically changes the consistency of the buttercream as well as the taste. Simply avoid them.

Gel and oil-based food colourings are the way forward, especially when working with buttercream. The intensity of the gel colouring means that a smaller amount is required and therefore goes a long way. The texture of these colourings works in harmony with the consistency of the buttercream and they mix in effortlessly.

When adding colour to buttercream, always start with a small amount and then add in more if you want a darker shade. While gel colouring is very concentrated in colour, different colours have different intensities. For example, I find that pink and blue colours are usually much stronger than yellows and greens. It depends on the brand you are using but, again, this is all about getting used to the ingredients that you have access to.

When decorating a cake, I like to leave 2–3 tablespoons of white buttercream to the side and colour the remaining buttercream. The white buttercream will be added to the cake at the end as a form of decoration, either left white or coloured with another shade to create some contrast with the rest of the cake.

When I add colour, I like to mix it in by hand using a spatula.

If you're mixing a large amount of buttercream, it can feel heavier and more difficult to mix in, so hold the spatula further down the handle.

I like to really beat the buttercream at this stage. Not only is this mixing the colour into the buttercream, it's also knocking out the air and making the buttercream smoother. I discovered this when I was making multiple cakes at the same time and some of the cakes were coloured and others were left white. I found that the coloured buttercream was always smoother than the white buttercream. I then realized it was because the coloured buttercream went through this extra stage of beating out the air. Therefore, nowadays, even if I want a white cake, I would still beat the white buttercream by hand before using it for decorating.

When it comes to cake decorating, I personally prefer pastel colours. I think there is something more natural looking about pastels and at the end of the day, you want the cake to look as appetizing as possible. I personally get put off by food that is a little bit too fluorescent!

Something to also get used to is the idea of mixing colours. Depending on the brand of colouring you are using, you may not love the shade that the colour provides directly from the bottle. For example, if you think the pink shade needs warming up, you can add a little bit of yellow to bring it to a warmer tone. I find that green colouring tends to come out quite bright, so I like adding a touch of blue colouring to make it look a bit more natural. Or, of course, if you want to make a totally new colour such as a peach or purple, then you can revisit your colour wheel from primary school and mix the colours together until your desired colour is formed. Colour mixing is part of the fun so get as creative as you like!

Applying a second coating of buttercream

Now we have our clean coloured or white buttercream ready to decorate our cake with, it's time to retrieve the cake from the refrigerator or freezer as well as all your equipment ready for the second coating of buttercream. Usually, by the time you've cleaned down your surface, coloured your buttercream and prepared for the second coating, the crumb coat should be fully set. I prefer using a piping bag to apply the buttercream in order to achieve an even amount of buttercream on the sides.

1 Fill a piping bag, about halfway, with the coloured buttercream.

2 Snip off the end (tip) of the piping bag 1cm/½in from the bottom.

3 Place your cake onto the turntable and double check the crumb coat layer has set (i.e. no buttercream stays on your finger to the touch).

4 Place the end of the piping bag next to the base of the cake where the cake touches the board and hold it at a 45° angle away from you, so you can see the hole at the end of the piping bag.

5 Start pushing the buttercream through the piping bag onto the cake and turn the turntable away from the piping bag, allowing a tube of buttercream to be piped directly onto the cake the same thickness as the hole of the piping bag.

If you hold the piping bag in your right hand, turn the turntable clockwise.

6 Once you've gone around the whole base of the cake, pipe another ring of buttercream around the cake just above the layer that you've just piped, making sure that the buttercream is pressed against the cake but still has the same thickness all the way around.

7 Repeat this process, piping the buttercream all the way up the sides of the cake until the very top.

8 When you reach the top, pipe one more ring of buttercream around the top corners.

9 Squeeze the remaining buttercream on the top of the cake. I usually pipe it in a loose spiral shape, not as tight as when we layered up the cake, but enough

Photo Steps Continue Overleaf _____

Top Tip

Smoothing can take anywhere between going six times around the cake to going 30 times around the cake. It all depends on experience and skill level, as well as how the buttercream reacts with the cake.

to fill up the majority of the top of the cake to make it easier to spread out.

If you run out of buttercream from your piping bag, you can fill it up at any point – if refilled, squeeze some out of the bag before you use it to get rid of any air bubbles.

10 With your palette knife, flatten out the top of the cake just as we did for the crumb coat. Firstly, spreading out the buttercream side to side using the outer edges of the palette knife, and then using one outer edge and turning the turntable to achieve a flat surface. This time we don't want the layer of buttercream to be as thin as before, so rather than pushing firmly down onto the cake, feel the resistance of the buttercream and glide the palette knife over, smoothing the buttercream out as we did when layering up our cake. If you push down too hard, you will take off too much buttercream and reveal the cake underneath. You're also aiming to almost push the buttercream over the edges of the cake so there is a slight overspill of buttercream. Once the top of the cake is smooth and flat, you won't be touching it until the very end.

Whenever you're applying a second coat of buttercream, the order is to start with the top of the cake, then smooth out the sides and then finish by cleaning off the corners. Every time you flatten out the top of the cake, the sides get affected. Every time you smooth out the sides, the top gets affected. This is why we decorate the cake in this order.

11 Now for the side scraper, only this time, we're going to refer to it as a SMOOTHER not a 'scraper' (as the action we want is more smoothing than scraping). The reason for this is that it's very common for people to get a bit carried away and scrape off too much buttercream from this layer. When placing the smoother against the cake, you want to hold it firmly in your hand but place it against the cake with a light touch.

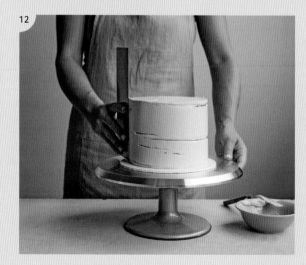

12 Keeping the smoother at the same angle as we did with the crumb coat, 45° towards you (not perpendicular to the cake), hand at the bottom of the smoother and the bottom edge touching the cake board, start turning the turntable. I like to begin by letting the weight of the smoother fall against the sides of the cake rather than pushing into the cake. Go around quite a few times to see how the buttercream reacts and redistributes.

The pressure against the cake is much less than it was for the crumb coat as we don't have the resistance and shape of the cake to guide us.

13 Once you've gone around the cake a few times, you will see that the gaps in between these piped layers of buttercream start to close. Now you can start to put a little bit more pressure onto the sides of the cake with the smoother. I go around the cake multiple times before I remove the smoother and wipe it clean from buttercream.

14 When the majority of the gaps between the layers of buttercream have closed, you can now check to see if any more buttercream needs to be added in certain places. Using the back of the palette knife, place on some excess buttercream over the areas that weren't caught by the smoother, then go over with the smoother one more time to even those areas out again.

15 When most of the buttercream is smooth but a few air bubbles remain, glide the smoother over the surface very gently, turning the cake in longer movements. Similar to how we smoothed out the crumb coat, come onto the cake with the smoother already in motion and lift the smoother off the cake while still turning the turntable to avoid any lines in the buttercream.

This is the hardest part of the cake to perfect. It takes years to perfect this layer of buttercream, so don't get frustrated if there are one or two air bubbles that won't go. You can always cover them up with the decorations!

Sharp corners

Even though most cakes are round, they still have corners where the sides of the cake meet the top surface. Back when fondant cakes headlined the industry, it was very common for cakes to have soft rounded corners. Nowadays, it's all about getting them as sharp and as angular as possible. Depending on the design of the cake, I choose which method of sharpening corners I use.

Firstly, it's important to understand how you make sure the corners are packed with buttercream in order to achieve a sharp clean finish. The number one rule is to keep your palette knife either horizontal along the top of the cake, or totally vertical against the sides of the cake. Never angle or curve your palette knife, especially over the corners, otherwise you will ruin the shape of the cake.

If you have smoothed out the buttercream on the sides of the cake, but the scraper didn't quite reach the very top edges, it means that there was not enough buttercream there to begin with. As tempting as it is to add on more buttercream just to the sides of the cake, adding buttercream on the top edge of the cake is equally as important. Remember when I mentioned to spread the buttercream on the top surface of the cake and to try and overspill towards the edges of the cake? This is to pack in the buttercream in the corners of the cake. So, if more buttercream needs to be added towards the top of the sides, start off by adding buttercream to the top of the cake, smooth it over with the palette knife and then go around the sides again. The smoother should catch the buttercream at the top of the cake and fill in those corners ready to be cleaned off.

QUICKER OPTION AND BETTER IF THEN ADDING OTHER DECORATIONS

1 Similar to the crumb coat and using one side of the palette knife holding it at an angle, glide from the outside of the cake into the centre, cutting off the excess buttercream at the top.

2 Wipe the palette knife clean from buttercream and repeat the same motion on the next section.

3 Continue all the way round the top corners of the cake until the corners are clean.

LONGER PROCESS BUT ACHIEVES SHARPER CORNERS

1 Place your cake in the refrigerator for at least 30 minutes or in the freezer for 10 minutes.

2 When the buttercream is completely hard, begin cutting away the excess buttercream using a small, sharp (paring) knife.

3 Start off cutting the corners gradually and taking off the excess buttercream that falls.

4 Cut the corners until the knife is flush against the top of the cake.

5 Clean any small remaining bits of buttercream with the palette knife.

The buttercream is hard at this point, so you can go over the cake with the side scraper without affecting the layer of buttercream. If coloured buttercream has been used, the colour may adjust slightly.

CAKE DECORATIONS

You've now learnt how to crumb coat, cover and smooth your buttercream cake. Usually, a centrepiece cake doesn't stop there. There are endless possibilities on how to transform a plain buttercream cake into a showstopper by adding all sorts of decorations on the top. Whether it's a more simple design, such as placing on fresh fruit, or something more technical, such as drips and shaped chocolate, the decorations are what makes the cake come alive and gives it a personality of its own.

I always say that once I teach someone the techniques of how to stack a cake correctly and smooth the buttercream out, I can't fully direct them on how to finish the cake because it's down to the individual and their eye for design. What I can do is guide them through the decorations I love to make, show which decorations I like adding to certain designs, and suggest how to arrange them on a cake as an example.

Drips

I remember when drip cakes became a trend. It was around the same time that I set up my Instagram account and I had the ability to follow other cake decorators from all over the world. There were a few cake designers based in Australia that caught my eye. Their cakes were totally over the top, adding all sorts of untraditional decorations on top, such as different candy bars, popcorn and chocolate drips. I absolutely fell in love with this concept and decided to try them out myself. The logic of dripping plain chocolate down a cake didn't totally make sense to me because chocolate hardens and can set cloudy if not tempered. I wanted to try a softer version, so I gave ganache a go. It worked like a treat and I've never looked back.

We've already covered how to make chocolate ganache (see pages 62–67); however, for dripping, the ganache needs to be a looser consistency so the recipe is slightly different.

Even though the quantities of cream and chocolate are different for drips, the method of making ganache is exactly the same as before. Please refer back to page 62 to see how to make ganache. Depending on the type of chocolate you use will affect the setting time of the chocolate and therefore the state and temperature of the cake differs. Here is a detailed guide on how to apply different colour/type of drips to your cake.

Chocolate drip ganache ratios

Whipping cream (36–38% fat)

SEMI-DARK CHOCOLATE (54%):
1:1 (75ml/2½fl oz/5 tbsp cream, 75g/2¾oz choc)

MILK CHOCOLATE (33%):
1:2 (50ml/1¾fl oz/3 tbsp cream,
100g/3½oz choc)

WHITE CHOCOLATE (28%):
1:3 (40ml/1½fl oz/2½ tbsp cream,
120g/4¼oz choc)

Double cream (42–48% fat)

SEMI-DARK CHOCOLATE (54%):
3:2 (75ml/2½fl oz/5 tbsp cream, 50g/1¾oz choc)

MILK CHOCOLATE (33%):
1:1 (75ml/2½fl oz/5 tbsp cream, 75g/2¾oz choc)

WHITE CHOCOLATE (28%):
1:2 (50ml/1¾fl oz/3 tbsp cream, 100g/3½oz choc)

Dark and milk chocolate drips

The most important factors when it comes to dripping chocolate are
to get the consistency of the ganache and the temperature of the cake
correct; however, it's not one way fits all. If the ganache is a slightly looser
consistency but the cake is cold, the ganache will set quickly. If the ganache
is slightly thicker but the cake isn't cold, the ganache will drip and set at
its own pace. So as always, it's getting used to your environment.

When I make dark or milk chocolate ganache, I keep the cake in the refrigerator
until I'm ready to drip. The ganache still retains some heat from the melting
process, but this is essential to ensure the ganache drips enough. If the cake
is at room temperature and the ganache is too hot, then the ganache can
melt the buttercream. I also make sure that the ganache is nice and loose,
similar to the consistency of runny honey, i.e. thick yet has movement.

When it comes to applying the drips, there are two methods I
like to use – I've explained these on the next few pages.

Palette knife

People think I'm crazy when I pour ganache over a cake and spread it out until it naturally falls over the edge, but I absolutely love this method. The organic fall of the chocolate, some drips longer than others and also that slight fear that it may not even work perfectly is what makes dripping the most exciting part! The motion is similar to how buttercream is spread on top of the cake; however, the consistency of the ganache and how it's moving is what determines how fast you need to work with it.

1 Make your ganache and refrigerate your cake for 5–10 minutes.

2 If the ganache is quite hot, leave it to cool slightly until it's warm to the touch.

3 Take your cake and place it back on the turntable and have the ganache and a clean palette knife ready to go.

4 Pour the ganache over the top of the cake until it fills about two-thirds of the surface.

5 Start spreading out the ganache using the palette knife while turning the turntable until it reaches the edges of the cake.

6 With the end of the palette knife blade, encourage the ganache to spill over the edge of the cake to begin forming drips.

The more you push over, the longer the drips. The runnier the ganache, the faster it will travel, so adjust the pressure and speed according to how it's reacting.

7 Once the ganache has been pushed over all of the edges, don't go over what you've already created as this can create an overlapping drip.

8 If there are large gaps where the ganache hasn't dripped, carefully add a small amount of ganache on the top of the cake just next to the edge and use the palette knife to let it fall over the corner.

9 Once the ganache sets, try not to spread over it again otherwise it will become textured rather than set smooth.

10 Leave the cake at room temperature for 15–20 minutes before refrigerating.

If you put ganache straight into the refrigerator, the harsh contrast in temperature may cause it to crack.

Piping bag

The main advantage of using a piping bag to drip the ganache is that you have more control over the amount of ganache dripping down the sides of the cake. It's definitely a safer option than the palette knife method; however, the overall effect is less organic as the drips tend to be the same length all the way round the cake. Some people prefer having the drips more evenly spaced and so this method is preferable to them. It's down to personal preference!

1 Make your ganache and refrigerate your cake for 5–10 minutes.

2 If the ganache is quite hot, leave it to cool slightly until it's warm to the touch.

3 Take your cake and place it back on the turntable.

4 Place a piping bag in a tall glass and fill the piping bag with the ganache (see pages 86–87 for more info on this).

5 Twist the top of the piping bag closed and cut a small hole off the end (tip) of the piping bag.

The ganache is loose, so once the bag is cut, hold the piping bag upside down to avoid the ganache coming out of the cut end!

6 Quickly turn the piping bag the right way round and try to 'land' on the top of the cake about 1cm/½in from the edge.

7 Let the ganache fall out of the piping bag rather than squeezing it out and move the piping bag towards the edge of the cake so the ganache starts to spill over the corner.

8 Once you're happy with the length of the drip you've created, move your piping hand(s) back away from the edge of the cake and move your hand(s) 2–3cm/¾–1¼in next to the drip you've just created, without lifting the piping bag from the surface of the cake.

9 Repeat the same process, moving the bag towards the edge of the cake until the ganache runs down the side.

You can control the amount of ganache coming out the piping bag by squeezing the bag more/less to achieve longer or shorter drips.

10 Once you've gone all the way around, fill up the centre of the cake either by squeezing the remaining ganache in a spiral towards the middle or spread it out with a palette knife.

Remember that the ganache will be setting on the cake, so try to work as quickly as possible as well as avoiding pushing any more ganache over the edge.

11 Leave the cake at room temperature for 15–20 minutes before refrigerating.

Top Tip

Decorations can be added when the ganache drips have just set, i.e. they are still soft enough to help the decorations stick to the ganache but are set enough so they don't get ruined. It's also possible to keep the dripped cakes in the refrigerator for a few hours or even overnight, if needed.

White chocolate drips

White chocolate behaves totally differently to dark and milk chocolate, especially in ganache form. Because of the high percentage of fat in white chocolate, it takes longer for it to set. Also, when chocolate is mixed with cream it becomes more yellow in colour, so in order to make beautiful white chocolate drips for your cakes, a couple of extra steps have to be taken.

Firstly, the cake has to be extremely cold in order for the white chocolate ganache to set quickly enough, otherwise it will continue dripping all the way to the bottom of the cake.

Before adding the drips, set the cake in the freezer for at least 20 minutes. If, like many people, your freezer doesn't have space for a cake, you can instead set your refrigerator to the lowest temperature and leave the cake to chill for at least 2 hours; however, the freezer always gives better results.

When white chocolate is mixed with cream, the ganache turns yellow. This is due to the high percentage of cocoa butter in the white chocolate. In order to make the ganache white again, a white food colouring needs to be added. However, normal gel food colouring cannot be mixed with white chocolate, otherwise it can split the chocolate, so we use something called titanium dioxide: a white powder which is used to whiten food. There are certain white chocolate food colourings that come in liquid form, but titanium dioxide is still the main ingredient. So whether you're using the powder or liquid form, ½ teaspoon or a few drops is mixed into the white chocolate ganache to bring it back to its original shade of white.

If using the powder, it won't mix into the chocolate completely and small lumps will still remain, so using a stick blender to combine the powder is essential.

1 Place your cake in the freezer for 20 minutes.

2 Make the white chocolate ganache as usual, mixing the chocolate and cream together until melted and combined.

Bear in mind that white chocolate has a lower melting point so it will take less time to melt than when making regular ganache.

3 Place the ganache into a bowl or a measuring jug and add ½ teaspoon of titanium dioxide powder (or a few drops of liquid titanium dioxide).

4 Using a stick blender, blend the ganache until the titanium dioxide has completely dissolved (or combined) and the ganache has whitened.

5 Take your cake from the freezer and apply the drips either using a palette knife or a piping bag (as explained on pages 122 and 124).

White chocolate drips fall slower than regular chocolate so if they don't fall quickly at first, wait a minute before adding more ganache if needed.

6 Place the cake in the refrigerator or back in the freezer for at least 10 minutes to set the white chocolate drips completely.

Coloured drips

Coloured drips are one step further than the process of creating white chocolate drips. I love colouring drips especially when I'm making a cake to suit a certain theme and the buttercream covering the cake is white. It adds a pop of colour and gives the cake character. Coloured drips are essentially white chocolate drips with added food colouring; however, just like the white chocolate, specific colouring has to be used otherwise it can split the chocolate.

Liquid and gel food colouring is water-based which can cause the chocolate to seize or split, so a powder or oil-based colouring is preferable when working with chocolate. Just like titanium dioxide for whitening (see page 126), there are many powdered food colourings that are specifically used for chocolate. Powder has a higher intensity of colour than gel colourings do, so bear that in mind when adding it to your ganache – remember to add colour gradually to achieve the desired intensity! Oil-based food colouring is also a safe option to use when mixing into chocolate, so use whatever you feel most comfortable with.

When I make coloured drips, I whiten the ganache before I add the colour, otherwise the ganache maintains a yellow tinge. So, in order to make coloured ganache, repeat the exact same process as for white chocolate drips on page 126, but just add colour after the titanium dioxide has been mixed in. Once again, if using a powder colour, the use of a stick blender is also advised in order to fully incorporate the powder.

Even though the drips are coloured, it is essentially white chocolate ganache, so the drips have to be treated in the exact same way – i.e. cold cake taken from the freezer and placed back in the refrigerator or freezer again to set. See the previous recipe for how to apply drips with a white chocolate base.

Metallic drips

After trying all of the shortcuts to create metallic drips, I always revert back to the longer process purely because it gives the best results. If only we could colour ganache a rich gold or silver and drip it down the cake! Unfortunately, the pigments don't work in that way. I create metallic drips by hand-painting edible lustre on top of white chocolate drips. It sounds like a lengthy process, but it is the only way to achieve shiny, clean metallic drips.

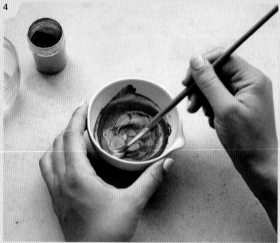

1 Make white chocolate ganache as normal but this time there's no need to add titanium dioxide, as with the white chocolate drips. The ganache will be yellow, but we're painting over it!

2 Apply the drips as before, either using the palette knife or piping bag method (see pages 122 and 124) and once finished, place into the freezer or refrigerator until the drips are completely set

It's very important that the white drips are fully set before painting on. I usually leave my cake with the drips to set for at least 1 hour in the freezer. Alternatively, apply the drips and leave the cake in the refrigerator overnight to ensure that the drips are fully set.

3 Metallic paint can be bought ready-mixed, or created from edible lustre dust and lemon juice or alcohol. Mix ½ teaspoon of edible lustre dust of your chosen colour with a teaspoon of vodka or lemon juice.

Don't worry about using vodka! The liquid eventually evaporates. Lemon juice works just the same!

4 In a small bowl, mix your dust and chosen liquid together until a thin paint consistency forms (you may need to adjust the quantities slightly depending on the type of lustre dust you use).

5 When the drips have set completely hard on the cake, remove it from the freezer/refrigerator and place back onto the turntable.

6 With a small, clean, food-safe paintbrush, begin painting on top of the drips using the metallic paint.

7 If the paint is a bit thin, add a small amount of lustre dust to make it thicker, and if the paint is still lumpy, add a few more drops of liquid and mix again before applying.

8 Continue painting until all the drips are covered in the metallic paint. Once the metallic paint is on, there is no need to chill the cake again before adding decorations. Just be aware that the paint is drying so try not to smudge it.

Top Tips

• The liquid will evaporate during the painting process not only on the drips but from the bowl as well, so you may need to continuously adjust the consistency of the paint by adding more liquid.

• If you accidentally paint the buttercream of the cake, take a clean food-safe paintbrush and clean the area (it comes right off as the buttercream has set completely).

• If you will be topping the cake with lots of decorations, then painting the whole top of the cake is unnecessary. Think of where your decorations will start and only paint up to that point on top!

Caramel drips

Caramel is the only other ingredient that I love dripping down a cake. Whether the cake inside is flavoured with caramel or not, I think that a caramel drip adds an indulgent aesthetic to a cake which makes it look even more appetizing. The caramel that I use for dripping is the exact same recipe as my caramel sauce that I use for filling a cake, too (see page 76). The only difference is that it's used at a different stage and consistency.

Once made, caramel sauce is very sensitive to temperature. If kept in the refrigerator, the caramel is thick and spreadable, whereas when it's heated, it becomes very loose. To create drips with caramel, similar to white chocolate ganache, it's best to have the cake at its coldest in order to set the caramel quickly (see page 126). Whether you're using freshly-made caramel sauce or taking it from a jar in the refrigerator, it has to get to the optimal temperature.

1 Place your cake into the freezer for 20 minutes.

2 If taking the caramel from the refrigerator, gently microwave or heat the caramel over a bain-marie until it begins to loosen. If freshly made, wait until there is hardly any heat remaining in the caramel sauce but it still retains a loose consistency (this may take a few hours).

3 Once the cake is cold, place it onto your turntable.

4 Apply the caramel drips using the palette knife or piping bag method (see pages 122 and 124). I personally prefer applying caramel drips with a piping bag. I find that with caramel drips they continue dripping for quite a while before completely setting, so bear this in mind when dripping with caramel. I usually aim to create shorter drips at first, which then become the length I like!

5 Once you're happy with your drips, place the cake straight into the refrigerator or back into the freezer.

6 Wait until the drips are completely set before taking the cake out of the refrigerator. The setting time can vary, but I usually allow 2–3 hours in the refrigerator or at least 1 hour in the freezer.

Meringue decorations

Believe it or not, if you've made Swiss meringue buttercream (see page 51), you've already made the same meringue for kisses and meringue lollipops. The process to make Swiss meringue suitable for piping is exactly the same process as for making Swiss meringue buttercream, just without the added butter. Swiss meringue is the best kind of meringue to pipe into shapes as it stays white, shiny and whisks up to a very stiff peak. Whether you choose to keep the meringue its natural white or add coloured stripes (as I explain in the method that follows) these crunchy sweet treats can suit any occasion! It's also just about the only gluten-free and dairy-free dessert I make which is always a winner!

The recipe for Swiss meringue is double the quantity of sugar to egg whites, and it works with any amount.

Makes 2 trays of piped meringue
(about 60 meringue kisses or about
20 meringue lollipops)

YOU WILL NEED
2 baking trays
baking paper or non-stick heatproof silicone mats
disposable piping bag
tall glass or bottle
food-safe paintbrush
paper lollipop sticks or paper straws

INGREDIENTS
100g/3½oz egg whites
200g/7oz/1 cup caster sugar
food colouring of your choice (I prefer to use gel
food colouring)

For the method of making Swiss meringue, follow steps 1–8 of the Swiss Meringue Buttercream recipe (see page 52) but using the ingredients above. You want this meringue to be at its stiffest peak, so whisk it for at least 5 minutes on the stand mixer. Now it's time to prepare a piping bag to pipe the meringue with. It's the same method for both kisses and lollipops.

1 Preheat the oven to 100°C/80°C fan/just below gas ¼ and line two baking trays with baking paper or non-stick heatproof silicone mats.

If using paper, dot a small amount of meringue in each corner between the paper and the tray to stick the paper down.

2 If you prefer to keep the meringue white, jump to step 8. If you want to create striped meringue, take a piping bag and place your whole hand inside the opening. Open your hand as much as you can and turn the piping bag inside out, leaving a small triangle at the end (tip) unturned – this will help you turn the bag the right way again later.

Photo Steps Continue Overleaf _____

3 Close the narrow end (where the small triangle is) of the piping bag as much as possible (about the width of a finger). Place the piping bag over a tall glass or bottle to free up your hands.

4 With a food-safe paintbrush and a small amount of food colouring, paint a line from the very tip of the piping bag where it's folded over the glass/bottle until about halfway down the bag.

When using colouring on the bag, it may look like not much is being applied because of the reaction with the plastic; however the colour is strong and one brush with colour is usually enough!

5 Think of how many colours you want to apply and paint 3–5 stripes of colour. When I'm using two colours, I paint on two stripes of each colour and alternate them around the piping bag. If I want a multicoloured effect, then I paint 5–6 stripes of different colours. It also works just fine with one colour, too!

I like to leave gaps in-between the lines because that's where the white meringue will show through and will create a nice contrast.

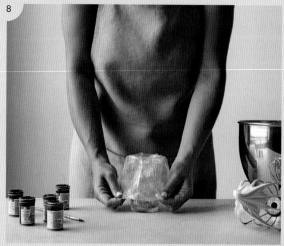

6 Once you've finished applying your colours, it's time to turn the piping bag the right way around again. Lift up the bag and reach inside to get hold of the small triangle that wasn't turned inside out.

7 In one movement, pull the small triangle through and it will turn the piping bag back the right way round again.

8 Place the piping bag in a tall glass and fold the top part of the bag down around the glass.

9 Fill the piping bag with meringue no more than two-thirds full and then remove the bag from the glass and twist the top closed.

10 If you are using colour, place the full piping bag on the work surface and stroke the meringue from the top of the bag to the bottom. This ensures that the meringue picks up the colour.

The meringue won't reach the bottom of the bag because it's not cut open yet.

Meringue kisses

Meringue kisses are little drops of heaven. Not only do they look beautiful as a cake decoration, they are also delicious to snack on! Meringue kisses are an excellent way to incorporate a touch of colour to suit a specific theme, whether as part of a cake or even displayed in a decorative bowl on a dessert table. These are my most popular cake decorations, purely because they're so easy to make and very versatile.

1 Cut the piping bag 2–4cm/¾–1½in from the end (tip) of the bag to make a hole.

2 Push the meringue through the bag until it reaches the opening.

3 Hold the piping bag perpendicular to a lined baking tray about 2cm/¾in from the surface of the tray, keeping the wider end/top of the bag twisted shut.

4 Push the meringue out of the bag with a strong force. As the meringue touches the tray, a ball of meringue should form.

5 Stop pushing the meringue through and then lift the piping bag upwards off the tray.

6 The meringue should narrow, break away from the bag and form a hook shape.

7 Continue piping kisses in the same way, leaving a couple of finger spaces between each kiss.

8 Bake the kisses in the pre-heated oven for 1–1½ hours at 100°C/80°C fan/just below gas ¼ until they're fully dried out and can be lifted off the tray easily. (*The size of the meringue kisses can affect the baking time.*)

Top Tip

You can buy non-stick heatproof silicone macaron mats, which already have the outlines of small circles marked on them to help when piping meringue kisses – these mats are not essential to use, but they do help as a guide!

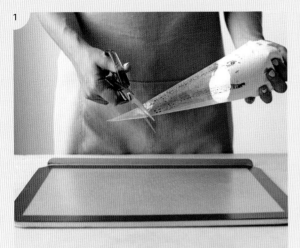

Things to note

- It's normal for the first few meringues to be stronger in colour than the rest.

- If you're too close to the baking tray, the meringue won't form a ball shape – it will be quite flat.

- If you're too far from the baking tray, the meringue will fall too far and be long and thin.

- If you continue to push the meringue while lifting up the piping bag, it will create more of a cone shape.

- The rhythm to repeat is: 'Push, stop pushing, then pull up'.

Meringue lollipops

I first came up with the idea of meringue lollipops when I was struggling to find large sugar lollipops to decorate my cakes with. Additionally, when I was lucky enough to find them, they were quite expensive. Meringue lollipops give the same effect as sugar lollipops without the cost and weight too (hard sugar can get heavy!). As always, the benefit of making something yourself is that you can adapt it to your needs, so if you wanted to match a specific colour theme, you can colour the meringue lollipops accordingly. These are definitely a favourite with kids too!

1 Cut the piping bag 1–2cm/½–¾in from the end (tip) of the bag to make a small hole. Push the meringue through the bag until it reaches the opening.

2 Pipe a small amount of meringue onto a lined baking tray and place a paper lollipop stick or paper straw on top.

This will hold the stick in place while you're piping.

3 Starting from one end of the stick/straw, pipe a spiral of meringue, starting from the inside and spiralling outwards.

4 To finish the spiral, stop pushing the meringue through the piping bag and rather than lifting upwards, flick the bag in the same direction as the spiral to tail off the lollipop.

If you're not happy with the finish, you can correct the ending by neatening it up with your finger!

5 Continue piping lollipops in the same way, leaving a few finger spaces in-between each one. I like piping them in alternative spaces so I can fit more on the tray.

6 Bake in the pre-heated oven for 1½–2 hours 100°C/80°C fan/just below gas ¼ until fully dried out and the lollipops can be easily lifted off the tray. (*The size of lollipops can affect the baking time.*)

There's no such thing as overcooking these meringues because of the very low temperature in the oven. The longer they're cooked, the drier the meringue. Cooked meringues are best eaten within 3 days but they will last for up to a week in an airtight container at room temperature.

Top Tip

If you want to make both meringue kisses and meringue lollipops (white or coloured), begin with the lollipops and then halfway through, cut the bag more to create a larger hole for piping kisses!

1

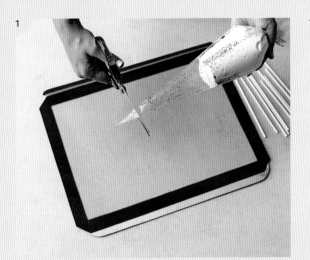

1

2

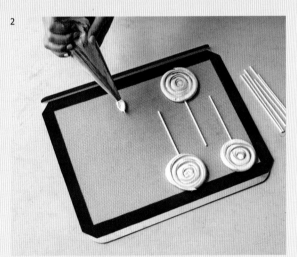

2

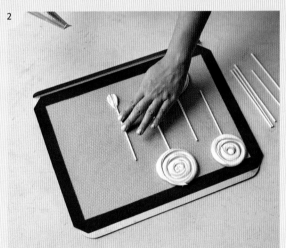

3

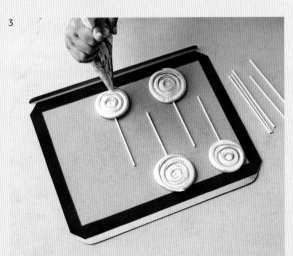

5

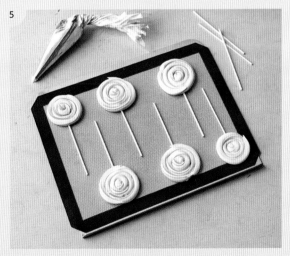

Making buttercream and extra meringue to pipe at the same time

Usually, I like to make a few meringue kisses or lollipops to decorate a cake so I don't always need to make one large batch of meringue. Additionally, if it's the exact same method for making the buttercream as it is for making meringue kisses, why do the same thing twice? I've developed the following method as an example of how to make buttercream and extra meringue to pipe at the same time.

NORMAL SWISS MERINGUE BUTTERCREAM QUANTITY
200g/7oz egg whites
400g/14oz/2 cups caster sugar
400g/14oz/1¾ cups unsalted butter

EXTRA MERINGUE QUANTITY
50g/1¾oz egg whites
100g/3½oz/½ cup caster sugar

TOTAL QUANTITY TO MEASURE OUT
250g/8¾oz egg whites
500g/1lb 1½oz/2½ cups caster sugar
400g/14oz/1¾ cups unsalted butter at room temperature, cut into cubes

To make the meringue, follow steps 1–8 for the Swiss Meringue Buttercream recipe (see page 52) and, once it's whisked to a stiff meringue, take out the extra meringue quantity that you added (i.e. 50g/1¾oz of egg whites and 100g/3½oz of caster sugar = 150g/5¼oz in total).

Once this 150g/5¼oz of meringue is taken out, the quantity of meringue remaining in the stand mixer bowl will return to the original buttercream recipe of 200g/7oz of egg whites and 400g/14oz of caster sugar to then match with the 400g/14oz of unsalted butter to be added to make the buttercream.

Troubleshooting

MERINGUE TOO SOFT? If the meringue has been whisking for 5 minutes and it's still a loose consistency, it's most likely that it was not heated enough at the beginning. Make sure it reaches a temperature of 65°C/149°F when cooking the egg whites and sugar over the water.

BROWN MERINGUE? Your oven temperature is too high! Even if the oven is reading 100°C/80°C fan/just below gas ¼, it may be too hot. Turn your oven down 10–20°C and, if needed, bake the meringue for longer.

CRACKED MERINGUE? Many factors can affect the cracking of meringue:

• Piping the meringue when it was too hot from the mixer.

• Leaving the meringue standing for too long before it's piped.

• Not all the sugar was dissolved in the egg white during the heating process.

• Inconsistent temperatures in the oven.

• Just bad luck!

I know the last point doesn't seem helpful, but sometimes baking disasters happen. Meringue is very sensitive and a tiny change in atmosphere, temperature or ingredients can create a huge difference. Try and get used to your equipment as much as possible, know your oven settings and most importantly, practise!

Dried fruit

I'm not one for traditional decorations on cakes, which is why I use dried fruit on the outside of the cake as part of the decorations rather than on the inside! I love the addition and versatility of dried fruit and it's so easy to make! I usually include dried fruits as part of the decoration to hint as to what flavour is inside the cake. For example, adding dried lemon slices to a lemon cake that's filled with lemon curd. But sometimes I just add them for fun!

Dried citrus fruit

Whether you're using lemons, oranges, grapefruits or limes, the process of making dried citrus slices is the same. The only thing that may vary is timings, and due to the varied amounts of sugar in the fruit, the end results will differ, so it's not 'one size fits all'.

YOU WILL NEED
baking tray and baking paper
sharp knife

1 Preheat the oven to 100°C/80°C fan/just below gas ¼ and line a baking tray with baking paper.

2 With a sharp knife, slice your chosen fruit into thin slices, approximately 2mm/¹/₁₆in thick.

The thicker the slices, the longer they will take to dry, so try and get them as thin as possible.

Photo Steps Continue Overleaf _____

143

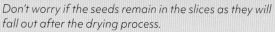

Don't worry if the seeds remain in the slices as they will fall out after the drying process.

3 Place the slices on some sheets of kitchen paper to soak up as much juice as possible.

4 Transfer the slices onto the lined baking tray and put the tray in the oven, then set a timer for 30 minutes.

5 Once the 30 minutes is up, take the tray from the oven and flip the slices over.

6 Place back in the oven for a further 30 minutes and repeat, flipping the slices again after the 30 minutes.

7 Depending on what fruit you've used and how thick/thin the slices are, start adjusting the intervals of the tray in the oven. If the slices are starting to dry after an hour, set the timer for 10 minutes each time and continue baking and flipping the slices until the slices are dry. If the slices are still full of juice, set a timer for a further 20–30 minutes.

8 You're looking for each slice of fruit to be dry and slightly translucent and to be able to be picked up and maintain its circular shape.

9 Sometimes certain slices dry quicker than others, so simply remove them from the tray and continue cooking the rest if needed.

10 Once baked, leave to cool completely on the baking tray (they will harden even more once out of the oven). For storage, see page 147.

Dried (eating) apples

From what I remember, dried apple slices were a happy accident when I was experimenting with different decorations. Fleshy fruits such as eating apples and pears dry completely differently to citrus fruit due to the different water contents and sugar levels. Once they're dry, the slices curl up and create these amazing organic shapes and they look so unique as part of the decorations on a cake. Citrus fruit has a wonderful natural colour that's retained when dry; however, apples tend to stay beige. Of course, their natural colour can work well depending on the look you're going for, but I find adding colour to the slices really exaggerates the shape.

YOU WILL NEED
mandoline
gel food colouring of your choice
disposable gloves (optional)
wire rack placed over a baking tray (optional)

1 Preheat the oven to 100°C/80°C fan/just below gas ¼ and remove the wire rack/shelf from the oven.

2 Using a mandoline, slice the fruit very thinly (there's no need to peel or core the apples as the pips will fall out naturally once the slices are dried).

If you don't have access to a mandoline, cut the fruit as thinly as possible with a sharp knife – about 1mm/ ¹⁄₃₂ in thick.

3 If leaving the apple in its natural colour, skip to step 6.

4 If colouring the apple, fill a bowl up with water and add 1–2 drops of gel food colouring, then mix until incorporated.

5 Dip the slices of apple into the bowl of coloured water, and leave them for a few seconds until the apple has absorbed the colour. It's optional to wear disposable gloves here to avoid staining your fingers!

I prefer making more pastel shades of colour, but if you want stronger colours, then add more colouring to the water.

6 Drain, then dab the slices with kitchen paper to soak up as much water as possible.

7 Place the slices directly onto the oven rack/shelf (or use a wire rack placed over a baking tray), spacing them apart.

8 Return the oven rack/shelf to the oven (or place the wire rack/baking tray on a shelf in the oven) and bake the fruit for 45–60 minutes.

There's no need to turn them, as the wire rack/shelf allows the fruit to dry from both the top and bottom.

9 Like the citrus fruit, baking times will differ depending on what kind and size of fruit you use. Once dry, remove from the oven and leave on the side to cool completely.

Storage

Dried fruit (citrus and apple slices) can be kept for up to a week in an airtight container at room temperature. If the fruit isn't dried completely, it is at risk of going bad, but on the other hand, if the fruit has completely dried out, then it will last much longer than a week.

Chocolate ruffles

I learnt how to make these ruffles when I studied patisserie at Le Cordon Bleu. We used them to decorate an elegant chocolate mousse and I fell in love with the technique, so it made sense for me to try them as decorations on a cake. People don't believe me when I say that there is no need for tempering chocolate during the process of making these ruffles; they're made by simply melting chocolate and then playing around with the temperatures (yes, that's different to tempering!). However, they can be temperamental and may take some practice. Even though I've made these time and time again, I still get misbehaving chocolate and have to be patient with the process.

Makes about 20 chocolate ruffles

YOU WILL NEED
saucepan
couverture chocolate chips (dark or white)
(or you can use a bar of chocolate, roughly chopped)
heatproof bowl (large enough to sit on the saucepan)
2 baking trays
large palette knife
wallpaper scraper
edible gold dust (optional)
food-safe paintbrush

1 Fill a saucepan halfway with water and place over a medium heat until steaming.

2 Add about 100g/3½oz of chocolate chips (or chopped chocolate) to a heatproof bowl and place the bowl over the saucepan.

3 Stir the chocolate with a spoon or spatula until the chocolate is completely melted, then remove the bowl from the water.

4 Turn a baking tray upside down so the underside is facing upwards.

5 Pour the chocolate onto the baking tray and spread it out thinly using a large palette knife. Try and smooth the chocolate as much as possible and as thinly as possible without it revealing the tray underneath.

6 Place the tray in the refrigerator for 5 minutes until the chocolate has clouded over.

7 Once the chocolate is just set to the touch, remove the tray from the refrigerator.

8 Using a (clean!) wallpaper scraper, place the scraper at one end of the tray and hold it at about a 20° angle from the tray. Scrape up the chocolate so it ruffles up the blade of the scraper and lift the scraper off.

If the chocolate cracks, leave it for 1–2 minutes longer to soften up.

9 Pinch the bottom of the ruffle together, remove it from the scraper and place it on another baking tray.

10 Repeat until all the melted chocolate is used up, playing around with the angles of the scraper to achieve more curved ruffles and even some rolled-up cigarillos.

If the chocolate no longer ruffles because it's too soft, place the baking tray back in the refrigerator for a couple of minutes.

11 Place the whole tray of ruffles in the refrigerator again for at least 20 minutes to allow the chocolate to set completely.

12 Once set, remove the tray and brush the ruffles with some edible gold dust using a food-safe paintbrush to enhance the shapes. Transfer the ruffles to an airtight container and keep in the refrigerator until you are ready to decorate the cake (or transfer them to a small plate, if using straight away).

Even though the chocolate isn't tempered, we're still playing around with the temperatures and therefore the chocolate does become more stable during this process. I would recommend making these ruffles as fresh as possible, maximum a day before decorating, as there is a risk of the chocolate blooming after a few days (blooming is where the fat separates leaving white patches on the surface).

Isomalt

I wouldn't be surprised if you've never heard of isomalt before. Isomalt is an artificial sugar alternative, but not one that is used in recipes as a replacement, more a decoration. Looking at the different sugar temperature stages (explained on page 18), 'crack' stage is when sugar is able to set in a clear form and can be moulded into shapes, such as sugar cages and spirals, to add as a decoration to plated desserts. The problem with using such sugar decorations on top of a cake is that sugar dissolves from moisture in the air within a short period of time. Isomalt can withstand moisture and other factors much more than sugar can, which is why it's a great ingredient to work with. While I wouldn't recommend eating a whole block of isomalt, it is edible, and like the rice paper (see page 158), creates some amazing abstract shapes, which can really transform your cake.

Isomalt comes in different forms: powder, small grains or even large, hard candy-like pieces. Whichever form you have access to, the process to prepare and create isomalt decorations is the same. While it may not be found in regular supermarkets, it can be easily found online or in specialized cook and baking shops.

Preparing isomalt

Like sugar, isomalt needs heating up until it has become a liquid form; however, unlike sugar, it doesn't burn or crystallize. Isomalt can also be melted in the microwave, but I prefer heating it in a saucepan so I can control the rate of it melting. For quantities of isomalt to use, see the sample decorations below.

YOU WILL NEED
isomalt
small saucepan
heatproof rubber spatula
gel food colouring of your choice
non-stick heatproof silicone mat
wooden or plastic pegs
tall glass and full water bottle
scissors

1 Add the weighed out amount of isomalt to a small saucepan and place it over a medium heat.

2 Leave the isomalt for about 5 minutes to start melting.

3 When parts of the isomalt are melting and turning into a translucent liquid, start moving it around with a rubber spatula to melt the crystals that have yet to catch.

4 Once the isomalt is completely melted, remove the pan from the heat.

5 Add a drop of gel food colouring and mix in until the whole pan is one even colour.

When the food colouring is added it will bubble quite vigorously. Warning – isomalt is very hot and can easily burn. Avoid direct contact with the skin and handle it with caution.

Here are a couple of different decorations you can make using isomalt:

Isomalt fan

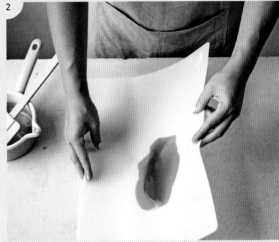

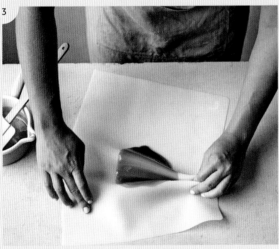

1 Melt 80g/3oz of isomalt as explained on page 154. Place a non-stick heatproof silicone mat on your work surface (or place it on top of a wooden chopping board to protect the work surface, if you prefer). Pour the melted isomalt onto the mat in a circular shape.

2 Lift up the mat and tilt it sideways, back and forth, so the isomalt falls back on itself and starts to slow down. Once the the consistency has become thicker, start to create a fan shape using the mat (without touching the isomalt itself because it's still very hot!).

3 Begin by folding a small section of the mat and pinching it closed. Bring a small section of the mat either side of the initial fold and gather it all on one side.

4 Secure the folds with wooden or plastic pegs and leave for at least 15 minutes to set and cool.

5 Once completely set, either lift up the isomalt fan directly from the mat or take the pegs away and carefully peel the mat away from the isomalt, revealing the fan.

Isomalt sail

1 Before melting the isomalt, prepare a tall mould: ideally, an upside down tall glass resting on a full water bottle to keep it weighed down. Place a non-stick heatproof silicone mat on your work surface (or place it on top of a wooden chopping board to protect the work surface, if you prefer).

2 Melt 120g/4¼oz of isomalt as explained on page 154, then pour the isomalt onto the silicone mat in a circular shape.

3 Lift up the mat and tilt it sideways, back and forth, keeping a circular shape until the movement of the isomalt starts to slow down (i.e. the consistency has become thicker).

4 When the isomalt looks thicker and is moving around less, place the mat on top of the glass mould, then let the mat drop and hang down the sides of the glass and let the isomalt start to flow down where the folds are.

Be aware of any dripping isomalt as it's still hot and some may drip off the mat.

5 Quickly peg the mat where the natural folds are so it holds its shape (using no more than 4–5 wooden or plastic pegs).

6 If there are any areas where the isomalt is dripping over the edge, wait a few seconds until it slows down, trim the trails with scissors and let the excess completely fall off the mat.

7 Leave to set and cool for at least 15 minutes.

8 Once set completely, unmould the isomalt by lifting it with the mat completely off the glass, holding it from the top.

9 Unpeg the mat and fold the mat inwards until the waves of the sail have released from the mat.

Sails are prone to breaking at this point!

10 Carefully lift the sail from the mat, turn it upside down so the flattest side is at the bottom and place it on the work surface.

Top Tips

• Isomalt is extremely fragile and can easily break, especially while unmoulding it from the mat. The wonderful thing about isomalt is that it can be easily re-melted. If your isomalt creation cracks or breaks, place the broken pieces back into the same saucepan that it was melted in. Re-melt the isomalt over a medium heat, then remove from the heat and create your decorations as before, with better luck this time!

• To clean the saucepan after the decorations have been made, pour boiling water into the pan and it will dissolve the isomalt.

• Isomalt decorations may start dissolving over time. Make the decorations no more than one day in advance and apply them to the cake as last minute as possible. Keep the isomalt fan or sail in an airtight container at room temperature if made in advance.

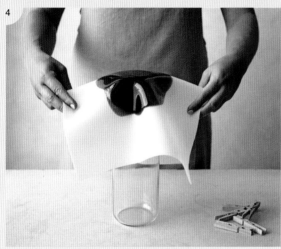

Rice paper sails

You're probably wondering why rice paper is included in this book. Usually used in Asian cooking, this ingredient is so versatile and can be moulded into the most incredible, abstract shapes (and you know very well by now that I'm all about making a cake look as abstract as possible!). When rice paper is dry, it's stiff and stable, whereas when it's wet, it's the most malleable, flexible material that we can use to our advantage. I probably wouldn't recommend eating it dry, but as far as decorations go, it is edible and makes such a statement on top of a cake.

YOU WILL NEED
gel food colouring of your choice
large deep plate or shallow bowl
rice paper
disposable gloves (optional)
non-stick heatproof silicone mat
ovenproof wooden pegs
baking tray

1 Preheat the oven to 80°C/60°C fan/below gas ¼ (lowest your gas oven can go).

2 Dilute some gel food colouring in water and pour it into a large deep plate or shallow bowl.

3 Take a piece of rice paper and place it into the water. Wait for about 30 seconds until the paper loosens up. It's optional to wear disposable gloves here to avoid staining your fingers!

4 Decide whether to use the whole piece of rice paper or smaller pieces (you can rip it at this point).

Photo Steps Continue Overleaf _____

5 Lift the rice paper from the water and let it drip for a few moments over the bowl.

6 Lay the wet rice paper onto a non-stick heatproof silicone mat.

7 Shape and fold the mat into any position or form you desire and keep it in place using ovenproof wooden pegs.

8 An alternative option is to mould the paper around a baking tin or ovenproof cup to create some more curved surfaces.

9 If you want to create many pieces, repeat the process with smaller or larger pieces of rice paper and place them onto the same mat (or use another mat as well) in different positions.

7

10 Place the mat onto a baking tray and place in the oven to dry out the paper. Rice paper usually takes around 45 minutes to dry out completely. If the paper has many folds, it may take longer.

The oven is at such a low temperature it's unlikely to over dry.

11 Once the rice paper is dry, take the tray out of the oven and leave the rice paper to cool completely and harden on the mat (on the baking tray) before unmoulding it from the mat.

The paper is delicate at this stage and can crack, so be gentle!

8

8

Top Tips

• It is also possible to leave the rice paper at room temperature to dry out (i.e. they are not oven-baked). This can be a lengthy process, as some pieces may take up to 4 hours to dry, which is why I prefer using the oven.

• You have the option to paint the edges of the rice paper with a metallic paint after baking, once the rice paper has hardened. Mix together vodka/lemon juice and edible lustre dust to form a metallic paint (see page 130) and brush it on the very edges of the hardened rice paper.

• Once dry, the rice paper can last for many weeks stored in an airtight container at room temperature. Once placed onto a cake and refrigerated, it may soak up some moisture over time, so try and add it to your cake as near to the last minute as possible.

Macarons

There are books, courses and lectures on learning how to make macarons. The process of making macarons is time-consuming, technical, and many factors can affect the outcome; however, they're one of my favourite decorations on a cake (and can also be a fancy sweet treat, too!).

Like with most of my recipes, it does come down to knowing your environment, ingredients and oven, etc.

A warm day, larger ground almonds and even a slightly uneven oven can all be factors as to why macarons may not work 100% perfectly, but I find my method to be the most efficient and reliable.

Macarons can be filled with any sort of buttercream or ganache, which have already been covered in this book (see pages 51 and 62), the technical bit is making the shells.

Makes about 60 sandwiched macarons

YOU WILL NEED
stand mixer with whisk attachment
small saucepan
bowl of water and a pastry brush
sugar thermometer
bowls
sieve
spatula
disposable piping bag
round piping nozzle/tip
tall glass
2–4 baking trays (or non-stick heatproof silicone macaron mats – see step 17)
baking paper
wire rack (optional)

INGREDIENTS
140g/5oz egg whites (weighed in two separate small bowls of 70g/2½oz each)
200g/7oz/1 cup caster sugar
50ml/1¾fl oz/3 tbsp water
200g/7oz/2 cups ground almonds
200g/7oz/scant 1½ cups icing sugar
gel food colouring of your choice

1 Put one of the bowls of egg whites into the stand mixer bowl with a whisk attachment but don't turn on.

2 Add the caster sugar and water into a small saucepan and place over a high heat. Heat the sugar and water until it reaches the 'soft ball' stage (116–120°C/241–248°F – I usually aim for 118°C/244°F).

Wash away any loose sugar crystals that may have come up the sides of the saucepan with water and a pastry brush.

3 Meanwhile, when the sugar reaches 110°C/230°F, start whisking the egg whites on a high-medium speed until they're thick and foamy.

4 When the sugar reaches the 'soft ball' stage (see Step 2), take the saucepan off the heat and turn the speed of the mixer down to medium-slow.

5 Slowly pour in the sugar syrup down the side of the mixer bowl.

Try not to hit the whisk with the sugar syrup to avoid getting splashes of sugar on the sides of the bowl.

6 Once all the sugar is inside, turn the speed back up to full speed and whisk until a thick meringue has formed and the bowl has cooled down significantly.

7 While the meringue is whisking, in a separate mixing bowl, sift together the ground almonds and icing sugar.

If there are large pieces of ground almonds that aren't passing through the sieve, weigh them in a separate bowl and replace them with additional finer ground almonds that pass through the sieve.

8 With a spatula, fold the ground almonds and icing sugar together until they're fully combined.

9 Add in the remaining 70g/2½oz measured egg whites and mix into the almonds and sugar until a very thick paste has formed.

10 By this point, the meringue should have whisked up to stiff peaks. Spoon about a third of the meringue into the almond mix and fold through until fully incorporated.

11 Add in half of the remaining meringue and fold in with a spatula until everything is incorporated. Add the remaining meringue into the almond mix and fold in until the meringue is only just incorporated.

12 If you are colouring the macarons more than one colour, divide the mix into as many bowls as you desire and add 1–2 drops of gel food colouring to each bowl.

13 Mix the colour through the macaron batter(s) and continue folding until you reach the 'ribbon stage'.

Ribbon stage is where you can lift up the batter with the spatula and drag it back over itself leaving a silky ribbon shape that takes about 6–8 seconds to disappear into the rest of the batter.

14 If using multiple colours, repeat this until all the colours are mixed in the separate bowls.

If just leaving the macaron batter white, fold the mix until the ribbon stage is achieved.

15 Prepare a piping bag with a round piping nozzle/tip. Place the piping nozzle/tip inside the bag and cut off the pointed end of the bag around the nozzle/tip, just below the opening. Twist the bag where the piping nozzle/tip is sitting and place the bag inside a tall glass, then fold the piping bag down over the sides of the glass.

16 Fill the piping bag with the macaron mix, then lift the bag from the glass and twist the top to keep it airtight.

17 Line 2–4 baking trays (depending on size) with baking paper by dotting some macaron batter in each corner of the tray under the paper to stick it down.

As mentioned earlier (when piping meringue kisses), you can buy non-stick heatproof silicone macaron mats, which already have the outlines of small circles marked on them to help when piping macarons – these mats are not essential to use, but they do help as a guide!

18 Now it's time to pipe the macarons. Hold the piping bag perpendicular to the baking tray, being cautious that the batter doesn't start falling out of the end.

19 Hover the bag 5mm/¼in above the baking tray (untwist the nozzle/tip end of the bag if it hasn't done this itself) and push the macaron batter through until a 2cm/¾in circle forms. Stop pushing the batter through and finish the circle off with a little flick of the piping bag to stop more batter from falling out of the bag.

20 Repeat until each tray is full, leaving a gap between each macaron. Once each tray is full, bang the tray on the surface to allow any air bubbles in the macarons to come to the surface.

You can also use a cocktail stick to burst any air bubbles that don't pop.

21 Leave each tray to dry at room temperature for about 20 minutes.

Photo Steps Continue Overleaf _____

You're looking for the shells to be dry to the touch. In warmer climates this may only take 10 minutes.

22 While the macarons are drying, preheat the oven to 155°C/135°C fan/gas 2.

23 Once the macarons are dry, bake them in the oven for 14–18 minutes until they have formed feet* around the bottom of each shell and have cooked through.

* Macaron feet are the textured surfaces that appear along the base of the macaron shells during the baking process. They are a good sign that your macaron batter was made correctly!

Only place up to two baking trays in the oven at one time. You may need to rotate your tray(s) after 10 minutes to maintain an even bake.

24 When the macarons are no longer soft, i.e. feel stiff to the touch instead of wobbling side to side, remove the tray(s) from the oven.

25 Carefully remove the paper (with the macarons still on it) from the tray(s) and leave the macarons to cool on the work surface or wire rack(s). Leave to cool completely before taking the shells off the paper.

26 Pair up the macaron shells and fill up a piping bag with a small round piping nozzle/tip with your chosen filling.

27 Pipe a small dome of filling onto the flat surfaces of one of the macaron shells until it fills two-thirds of the surface.

28 Place the other macaron shell on top of the piped filling with the flat surface facing down and squeeze the shells together until the filling reaches the outside edges.

29 Repeat until all of the macarons are filled and then set in the refrigerator for at least one hour before handling/serving.

I like to make a large batch of macarons and then freeze the shells without filling them. I then take out however many I need for one cake at a time. Filled macarons can keep up to one week in the refrigerator, and both filled and unfilled macarons can keep up to three months in the freezer.

Troubleshooting

UNDERCOOKED MACARONS? This is where I stress that you need to know how your oven behaves. If the macarons lose their base as you lift them from the baking paper, it's most likely that they need an extra couple of minutes in the oven. Alternatively, you can leave them to cool completely (on the paper) on the baking tray, rather than taking the paper off straight away (with the macarons in place) as above, in order to cook the bases a little further.

EXPLODED MACARONS? One or two macarons may have cracked during the baking process and look like they've exploded from the inside. This is most likely due to a large piece of sugar in the batter. To avoid this, when incorporating the meringue into the almond paste, make sure you're not scraping off any hardened sugar that may have fallen onto the sides of the mixer bowl.

NO FEET TO THE MACARONS? Either your oven wasn't hot enough for the macarons to get that initial rise or the macarons were dried for too long before baking. If the feet aren't forming in the first 6–8 minutes of baking, then they probably won't form much more if at all.

COMPLETE FAILURE? You're not alone! As I mentioned, macarons are tricky little treats that take years of practice and perfecting. I still get a batch here and there that don't turn out exactly how I'd hoped. Every step of the process has a small risk of causing a failed macaron batch, so trust your baker's instinct and be confident!

Fresh and edible flowers

Flowers are one of the most traditional decorations for celebration cakes, especially for weddings. Their natural forms, colours and even aromas add such beauty and elegance that no hand-made decoration can ever match up to.

There is sometimes confusion as to whether or not fresh flowers should be used on cakes, as not all flowers are edible. There are specific edible flowers that are available to purchase which have been grown organically and are safe to use on food. Non-edible or regular store-bought flowers can, in fact, be used on food, or in this case, cake, if prepared correctly.

Pansies and violas are the most readily available edible flowers, whereas specific farms and companies offer a wider variety. These flowers have been grown without using any chemicals or pesticides, making them safe for consumption, and they can therefore be added to cakes directly (or any food for that matter!).

When I want to add flowers among other decorations, I usually opt for the smaller varieties and use them to fill in any gaps and bulk out the design. If the cake is minimalistic and I want the flowers to be the focus, I would use larger flowers and create more of a bouquet as a centrepiece on top of the cake.

Fresh flowers

Celebration cakes for weddings and larger parties usually require matching flowers with the event's decor. Therefore, it is typically preferred to use regular store-bought flowers rather than specifically grown edible ones. Unlike the organically grown edible flowers, these have been treated with certain chemicals and are not recommended to have direct contact with the cake. Nevertheless, there are a few ways of how to prepare these flowers in order to safely place them on a cake.

YOU WILL NEED
fresh flowers of your choice
scissors
wooden cocktail sticks
florist tape
paper or plastic straws

1 Cut the stems of your flowers to about 2.5cm/1in below the flower heads using scissors. If you are using foliage, decide how much you want on the cake and cut accordingly, removing the last couple of leaves so at least 2.5cm/1in of the stem remains at the bottom.

2 Take one of your flowers and place a wooden cocktail stick at the end of the stem.

3 Wrap some florist tape around the base of the stem and the top of the cocktail stick to bind them together.

Florist tape gets sticky by stretching it and by rubbing it in the heat of your hands.

4 Repeat for different varieties and combinations of flowers.

5 Take one of the taped flowers or foliage and cut a paper or plastic straw to almost match the length, leaving 1cm/½in of straw below the end of the stem.

6 Insert the taped flower or foliage into the paper or plastic straw.

7 Repeat for all of the taped flowers or foliage. You can also create small bunches of several flowers using the same method. All the stems need to be able to fit inside the straw though so this works best with smaller flower heads and foliage with more delicate stems.

When it comes to decorating your cake and inserting the flowers, the straws will protect the cake from touching the flowers, as well as the florist tape, which keeps them secure. You can prepare these flowers one day before decorating your cake, if kept refrigerated.

CAKE DESIGNS

In this chapter, I will guide you through some of my signature
designs that involve my favourite techniques with the application
of buttercream, as well as explaining how to finish off your cakes to
the highest level starting with a simple crumb coat. By the end of this
chapter, you will have the knowledge of how versatile buttercream can
be as well as the confidence to work with it in your own ways.

All of the following designs begin with a crumb-coated cake. Please
refer back to chapter four (page 80) to see how to get to this stage.

NAKED CAKE

174

WATERCOLOUR
BUTTERCREAM CAKE

178

TEXTURED
BUTTERCREAM CAKE

182

OMBRE
BUTTERCREAM CAKE

186

STRIPED
BUTTERCREAM CAKE

191

CANDY LAND
SPRINKLES CAKE

196

Naked cake

Even though I think the word 'rustic' is very much overused, a naked cake is exactly that. Naked cakes took the industry by surprise because never before had anyone seen 'unfinished cakes' as a centrepiece. A true naked cake is where the sides of the cake are totally exposed so the layers of buttercream can be seen from the outside. In my opinion, sponge cake can dry out very quickly if it's exposed to air, so when I made my first naked cake I left a thin layer of buttercream around the outside of the cake. It was pretty much a refined crumb coat, so I adopted the name 'semi-naked cake'.

While this design is not a true naked cake, I love the balance between the amount of buttercream and the exposed cake from a visual perspective, but it also prevents the cake from drying out so it remains as tasty as possible. Even though it looks just like a crumb coat, there is an extra step in order to get a flawless looking semi-naked cake effect. Pretty much any decoration suits this style of cake, but due to its rustic nature, I love keeping the decorations simple with some dried or fresh fruit and fresh flowers.

Swiss meringue buttercream quantities for a naked cake:

15CM/6IN CAKE
150g/5½oz egg whites;
300g/10½oz/1½ cups caster sugar;
300g/10½oz/1⅓ cups unsalted butter

20CM/8IN CAKE
200g/7oz egg whites;
400g/14oz/2 cups caster sugar;
400g/14oz/1¾ cups unsalted butter

25CM/10IN CAKE
250g/9oz egg whites; 500g/1lb 2oz/
2½ cups caster sugar; 500g/1lb 2oz/
scant 2¼ cups unsalted butter

1 Starting from the crumb coat stage, take your cake out of the refrigerator or freezer, place it onto the turntable, then use the back of your palette knife to spread a thin layer of buttercream around the outside of the cake, just like we did for the original crumb coat.

Photo Steps Continue Overleaf _____

174

2 Place about a teaspoon of buttercream on the top of the cake and spread it out thinly using the palette knife.

3 Use one edge of the palette knife angled away from you and rotate the cake until the buttercream has smoothed out and pushed out towards the top edges.

4 Using the side scraper, smooth out the sides of the cake. Because it's a semi-naked cake, you can apply more pressure against the cake than if it were a thicker second coat of buttercream. This thin layer of buttercream will fill in any small holes that weren't filled in the crumb coat stage, therefore making the crumb coat look neater and more refined.

5 Finish this stage by cleaning off the top corners where the buttercream has moved upwards, using the edge of the palette knife and moving the excess buttercream towards the centre of the cake.

6 Set the cake in the refrigerator while you prepare the decorations: I love pairing a naked cake with dried lemon slices and fresh flowers (see pages 143 and 170).

Setting the cake in the refrigerator will harden the buttercream and protect it when adding the decorations.

7 When decorating a cake, it's important to choose your front. Ideally, the 360° view of the cake should be as perfect as possible, but we're only human! There will always be one side of a cake that looks a fraction better than the rest.

8 Once you have chosen your front, add the decorations accordingly. Naturally, I place the decorations on the top of the cake to one side and then add a small collection of decorations at the bottom of the cake on the opposite side to balance the overall look. I always recommend decorating the cake in the way that feels natural to you.

9 I begin by adding the larger decorations, in this case the flowers, and then the smaller dried lemon slices in between. To add the flowers, insert one of the stems prepared earlier (see page 170) and press it down into the cake until the straw is no longer visible.

10 Build up the flowers on top of the cake by arranging the individual stems or bunches, if you've made them (see page 170 for how to make bunches).

11 To add the dried lemon slices, add any remaining buttercream to a piping bag and pipe on a small amount where you want to add the slices.

Buttercream works as an adhesive for decorations. Either cut the hole in the end (tip) of the piping bag very small so this excess buttercream is hidden underneath the decorations, or use a small piping nozzle/tip and make the buttercream part of the design.

12 For the side of the cake, repeat the same process with the flowers and dried lemon slices. Insert the straw sideways each time followed by the flowers.

13 To finish the cake, I add a touch of edible gold leaf and edible glitter, which is again completely optional. Gold leaf is extremely delicate, so it's best to use a food-safe paintbrush to apply it. Carefully lift the gold leaf from the sheet it's packaged in and brush it against the buttercream to stick it down.

Because the buttercream is soft, the gold leaf adheres to it easily.

14 Sprinkle a light dusting of edible glitter to finish the cake!

Top Tips

• Store the cake in the refrigerator until 1–2 hours before serving (the idea is to serve the cake when the buttercream has softened a little, but it's also down to personal preference, as the cake is easier to cut when cold).

• Insert the flowers onto the cake as last minute as possible so they say fresher for longer (the flowers can be kept on the cake in the refrigerator and they will remain fresh, but if the cake is standing at room temperature for a few hours, it's best to place them on as late as possible).

Watercolour buttercream cake

A block colour on a cake can be quite overpowering if you're after something more delicate. Introducing watercolour buttercream. After experimenting with this technique multiple times, I found that this technique works best when one colour is used against a white background. If too many colours are introduced then it can look quite busy and take away from the subtlety that watercolour buttercream achieves. This is one of my favourite buttercream effects for more sophisticated events, such as weddings, where the majority of the colour scheme is usually white. I love decorating this cake with a white chocolate drip and delicate decorations on top.

Swiss meringue buttercream quantities for a watercolour buttercream cake:

15CM/6IN CAKE
200g/7oz egg whites;
400g/14oz/2 cups caster sugar;
400g/14oz/1¾ cups unsalted butter

20CM/8IN CAKE
250g/9oz egg whites; 500g/1lb 2oz/
2½ cups caster sugar; 500g/1lb 2oz/
scant 2¼ cups unsalted butter

25CM/10IN CAKE
300g/10½oz egg whites;
600g/1lb 5oz/3 cups caster sugar;
600g/1lb 5oz/2¾ cups unsalted butter

1 Crumb coat your cake and put it in the refrigerator or freezer until the buttercream has set hard.

2 In a small bowl, mix 2–3 tablespoons of buttercream with a little gel food colouring of your choice (it's best to start with a small drop of colouring and mix it in, then if you want a stronger colour, you can add in more colouring, drop by drop) and fill a piping bag with most of the remaining white buttercream (set aside about 1–2 tablespoons).

Photo Steps Continue Overleaf _____

3 Complete steps 1–10 from 'applying a second coating of buttercream' (see page 110) using the white buttercream in the piping bag.

4 Begin smoothing out the top of the cake with a palette knife and the sides of the cake with the side scraper.

5 Stop smoothing the sides just before you're happy with the finish, as now is the time to add on the colour for the watercolour effect.

6 With the end of the palette knife, take a very small amount of the coloured buttercream and place it onto the side of the cake.

7 Repeat all around the sides of the cake, as well as the top, leaving a couple of 2.5cm/1in gaps between each 'dot' of colour (you'll use around 1 tablespoon or so of the coloured buttercream for all this).

8 Begin spreading out the buttercream as usual on the top of the cake using the side of the palette knife and turning the turntable. The colour will start to blend into the white buttercream.

9 Once the top of the cake is smooth, begin smoothing the sides of the cake with the side scraper, once again blending the colour with the white buttercream.

10 Smooth the cake until the buttercream has blended and you're happy with the finish.

Top Tips

• Match the colour of your decorations with the colour of the buttercream to tie the cake together.

• This buttercream also works beautifully with darker chocolate drips or even no drips at all.

11 Clean the top corners using the palette knife and then place the cake in the freezer to firm up in preparation for the white chocolate drips.

12 Prepare some white chocolate ganache (see page 62) for dripping and apply to the cake as shown on page 124.

It is also an option to apply the white chocolate drips to just one side of the cake rather than the whole way around.

13 Insert a small star piping nozzle/tip in a piping bag and cut off the end to expose the nozzle/tip.

14 Place the piping bag into a tall glass and fold the top of the bag down over the sides of the glass.

15 Spoon in both the remaining coloured buttercream and a similar amount of the remaining (reserved) white buttercream (that you set aside in step 2), spreading each colour up opposite sides of the bag.

16 When the bag is lifted from the glass and twisted closed, the two colours will come through the piping bag at the same time.

17 Use this buttercream to map out where you want to place your decorations on top of the white chocolate drips. Squeeze the buttercream onto the top of the cake in star shapes and swirls to create a textured area, which will adhere the decorations.

18 Place your chosen decorations on top of the piped buttercream; for example, meringue kisses, chocolate ruffles and macarons (see pages 138, 149 and 162).

19 Fill the gaps in-between the decorations with small edible flowers and add a touch of edible glitter to finish.

See page 212 for information on storing a decorated cake.

Textured buttercream cake

There are many reasons why I enjoy using Swiss meringue buttercream more than other fillings and creams: it's delicious to eat, holds up a cake strongly and smooths out perfectly. Another reason is the versatility of the buttercream and the way it reacts to temperatures, which can result in some amazing effects.

As you have learnt from previous sections in this book, buttercream sets in the refrigerator or freezer and becomes hard. If we take advantage of this reaction, we can start building up texture using the buttercream and create some really interesting and abstract designs.

When the buttercream has a busy design, such as different colours and textures, I usually minimize the decorations on top, otherwise it can look a bit too overboard (yes, that is a thing!), so I tend to team textured buttercream with an abstract isomalt sail (see page 156).

(see page 156)

> ## Swiss meringue buttercream quantities for a textured buttercream cake:
>
> ### 15CM/6IN CAKE
> 200g/7oz egg whites;
> 400g/14oz/2 cups caster sugar;
> 400g/14oz/1¾ cups unsalted butter
>
> ### 20CM/8IN CAKE
> 250g/9oz egg whites; 500g/1lb 2oz/
> 2½ cups caster sugar; 500g/1lb 2oz/
> scant 2¼ cups unsalted butter
>
> ### 25CM/10IN CAKE
> 450g/1lb egg whites;
> 900g/2lb/4½ cups caster sugar;
> 900g/2lb/4 cups unsalted butter

1 Cover your cake in a second layer of buttercream and put the cake in the freezer (preferably) for 15–20 minutes (or in the refrigerator for at least 1 hour) until the buttercream has set hard.

2 Take your remaining buttercream and divide it into three bowls.

Photo Steps Continue Overleaf _____

182

3 Decide whether you want to colour this buttercream three shades of the same colour, or different colours all together. Add 1–3 drops of gel food colouring to the bowl(s) of buttercream and mix it in (the amount of colouring you add depends on the intensity of colour required – always start with less colouring than you think and then add more, if needed).

I love the contrast of different shades of the same colour, but it works equally well with different colours to complement the theme of a cake, too.

4 When the cake has set hard and cold, place it back onto the turntable.

5 Begin with the lightest shade of colour and apply a small amount (1–2 teaspoons at a time) of that coloured buttercream onto the back of the palette knife.

6 Lightly swipe the palette knife over the surface on one side of the cake in one motion, spreading out the small amount of buttercream.

7 Repeat with the same colour in a different area on the side of the cake or even changing direction.

You can spread the buttercream sideways across the side of the cake, or vertically down the side.

8 Once you are happy with the coverage of the first colour, switch to another colour or shade and repeat the same. Because the cake is cold, the buttercream would have already set hard so you can overlap the coloured buttercream already placed on the cake.

9 As you apply more buttercream, you will start to notice more texture and layers being built up.

10 Finally, apply the last colour or shade in smaller areas, again, on top of the buttercream that is already on the cake.

The darker shade or colour can easily override the other shades, so go on with a bit less than the first colour(s).

11 If you want to spread the buttercream out even more, you can use the palette knife and gently move the coloured buttercream around the cake.

12 If at any point the buttercream starts to soften and you want to create more texture, place the cake back in the freezer for 5–10 minutes (or in the refrigerator for about 1 hour), then continue once it has set hard again.

13 Repeat the same technique on the top of the cake to continue the design.

Or you can leave the top untextured!

14 Finish the cake off with an eye-catching decoration, such as an isomalt sail (see page 156).

15 To attach the isomalt sail (or other decoration) to the cake, take a small amount of buttercream and spread it on top of the cake in the centre. Place the flat side of the isomalt sail (or other decoration) on top of the cake and press down until secured.

See page 212 for information on storing a decorated cake.

Top Tips

• If I'm adding texture to a cake, I usually start with a white buttercream base and then add colour on top. If you want to use a coloured buttercream as the base layer, I would recommend opting for a light shade so there is contrast with the texture on top. It's easy to get carried away and add a lot of colour and textures, but remember that colours tend to overpower white and so the white can easily get lost. Build the layers and colours up gradually.

• If you are using an isomalt sail, attach it to the cake as last minute as possible to avoid it getting sticky!

Ombre buttercream cake

Ombre, meaning 'shaded' in French, refers to the gradual blending from one colour to another. Either from a darker to a lighter shade or different colours completely. As far as cake decorating goes, creating an ombre buttercream is a unique way to incorporate a colour and a theme into your cake. I love playing around with different colour and shade combinations, and even apply an ombre effect over a few tiers when making a larger stacked cake. The way to create an ombre effect has a similar application to the Striped Buttercream Cake (see page 191) but with an extra few steps.

(see page 191)

Swiss meringue buttercream quantities for an ombre buttercream cake:

15CM/6IN CAKE
250g/9oz egg whites; 500g/1lb 2oz/ 2½ cups caster sugar; 500g/1lb 2oz/ scant 2¼ cups unsalted butter

20CM/8IN CAKE
350g/12oz egg whites; 700g/1lb 9oz/3½ cups caster sugar; 700g/1lb 9oz/3 cups unsalted butter

25CM/10IN CAKE
450g/1lb egg whites; 900g/2lb/4½ cups caster sugar; 900g/2lb/4 cups unsalted butter

1 Crumb coat your cake and put it in the refrigerator or freezer until the buttercream has set hard.

2 Take the remaining buttercream and mix it by hand until it becomes smooth and less aerated.

3 Place 3 tablespoons of the buttercream into a small bowl and add 3–5 drops of gel food colouring. This will be your darkest shade of the cake so bear that in mind!

Photo Steps Continue Overleaf _____

4 Once the buttercream is coloured, fill a piping bag with that buttercream and cut a small hole off the end (tip) of the bag.

5 When your crumb coat has set in the refrigerator, place the cake back onto the turntable. Then, just like in our striped buttercream cake, pipe two narrow rings of buttercream around the base of the cake, keeping the thickness as even as possible.

6 Once the two lines of buttercream have been piped on, empty the piping bag into the same bowl that it was coloured in.

7 Add a heaped tablespoonful of white buttercream to the coloured buttercream and mix in thoroughly – the shade of colour should become a little lighter.

8 Place the buttercream back into the same piping bag and pipe another two rings of buttercream onto the cake, just above the previously piped ones.

9 Once again, empty the buttercream from the piping bag into the bowl, add another heaped tablespoonful of white buttercream and mix in thoroughly – the shade should become a little lighter again.

10 Refill the piping bag and pipe on a further two rings of buttercream around the cake.

11 Repeat this same process until you reach just under the very top of the cake – the shades of colour will have got lighter all the way up the cake.

You can use a new disposable piping bag each time for piping on each pair of coloured rings, but I like using and refilling one bag to mix the shades in the bag and add to the overall effect. It can get a bit messy, but do persevere using just the one bag if you can! It also saves on the cost of using multiple bags!

12 For the top, fill a new piping bag with plain white buttercream and pipe white rings around the top edge, as well as covering the very top of the cake, too.

13 Now it's time to blend these shades! If not, then stripes will form. Using the back of your palette knife, horizontally, rub in a circular direction where the first two shades meet (towards the bottom of the cake), blending the shades of buttercream together.

It will look like you're ruining the cake, but this is how we achieve a blended effect rather than a striped one!

14 Work your way up the whole cake in the same way, blending in each layer to the next, including the lightest shade with the white buttercream at the top.

15 Once the sides are shaded, smooth out the top of the cake using the palette knife.

16 Now begin smoothing out the sides of the cake using the side scraper. You will see how the shading will neaten up and become more apparent.

17 Don't clean your scraper until all air pockets and gaps have been filled, so that you can use the excess buttercream from the scraper, as this will have the exact shade of colour you need. Otherwise you won't have it at all!

18 Continue smoothing around the sides of the cake until you're happy with the final finish.

19 Of course, this cake can be decorated in many different ways. I like to pair up an ombre cake with delicate white chocolate drips, chocolate ruffles, macarons and dried fruit (see pages 126, 149, 162 and 143) for a summery feel!

20 Any leftover buttercream can be added to a piping bag fitted with a small star piping nozzle/ tip to then used for placing on decorations and adding details.

See page 212 for information on storing a decorated cake.

Striped buttercream cake

Even though it feels like rainbows and unicorns have been around forever, a rainbow-striped cake is still one of my favourite buttercream designs to make, purely because it's colourful and fun! Whether you pair this buttercream design with minimalistic decorations or go all out and make something crazy, having a colourful base will always scream out 'showstopper'.

The same technique can be applied using any colour combinations. I'm going to use several colours to explain how I decorate my own take on a 'rainbow' cake.

Obviously, the rainbow consists of seven colours; however, I limit it to five and keep it pastel. I would rather have fewer colours and make more of an impact with each of them than try to cram them all onto one cake.

Swiss meringue buttercream quantities for a striped buttercream cake:

15CM/6IN CAKE
250g/9oz egg whites; 500g/1lb 2oz/ 2½ cups caster sugar; 500g/1lb 2oz/ scant 2¼ cups unsalted butter

20CM/8IN CAKE
350g/12oz egg whites; 700g/1lb 9oz/3½ cups caster sugar; 700g/1lb 9oz/3 cups unsalted butter

25CM/10IN CAKE
450g/1lb egg whites; 900g/2lb/4½ cups caster sugar; 900g/2lb/4 cups unsalted butter

---

1 Crumb coat your cake and put it in the refrigerator or freezer until the buttercream has set hard.

2 Divide your remaining buttercream into five bowls.

3 Using 1–2 drops of gel food colouring for each bowl, colour the buttercream pink, yellow, green, blue and purple. The number of drops of colouring you add to each bowl will depend on the colour choice and intensity (yellow is stronger than purple, for example).

I like to keep the colours pastel. It's very difficult to achieve a red buttercream, which is why I opt for pink!

4 Fill up five piping bags with each of the colours and cut a small hole off the end (tip) of each one.

5 Take your cake from the refrigerator and place it back onto the turntable.

6 Arrange your colours on the work surface in the order in which you would like to use them.

I like to start with the purple and work backwards to end with the pink at the top.

7 Before applying the colours, roughly mark out five even sections down the side of the cake where each colour will fill. I usually do this by eye, but feel free to measure using a ruler, if you prefer!

8 Take your first colour and place the piping bag at the bottom edge of the cake, angled slightly away from you.

9 Begin turning the cake and squeezing out the buttercream so a clean tube of colour comes out of the end of the piping bag onto the cake. Continue this action until you have piped a ring of buttercream around the base of the cake.

Photo Steps Continue Overleaf _____

10 Apply a second ring of the same coloured buttercream on top of the one you have just piped, so there are two layers of the same colour on top of each other.

This is where you need to judge how thick to pipe your buttercream on the cake. It depends how tall the cake is and how large you cut the hole at the end of the piping bag. Sometimes you need three rings of each colour, sometimes one is enough.

11 Take your next colour and repeat the same process, piping the first ring on top of the first colour, and then apply a second ring of buttercream on top of the first ring of the same colour.

Don't worry if there are small gaps between the colours, as they will fill in themselves when we scrape. If there are larger gaps, then fill these up with more buttercream.

12 By the time you are using your third colour, you should be about halfway up the cake.

13 Repeat the process with the remaining two colours, and with the last colour, pipe until the very top of the cake is also covered.

14 Depending on the decoration you're choosing, decide whether to completely cover the top of the cake with buttercream or leave it as a thin layer.

If you're applying drips, you don't necessarily have to cover the whole top with buttercream as it will be covered in chocolate.

15 As before, flatten the buttercream on top of the cake using your palette knife. Use the side of the blade to smooth out the top of the cake while turning the turntable.

16 Use the palette knife to push the buttercream slightly over the edge to ensure that the corners are filled with buttercream.

17 Once you're happy with the top of the cake, it's time for the side scraper. With a very light pressure, come onto the cake with the side scraper and begin slightly pushing the buttercream into the cake while turning the turntable.

18 It's very important to go around the cake multiple times to let the stripes of buttercream appear before you come off with the scraper.

If one colour was piped on thicker than the other, it may start to overlap another colour. If this happens, clean your scraper of excess buttercream sooner and continue smoothing.

19 If there are gaps between the colours, they should close as you smooth over with the scraper. Of course, if the gaps are too large, you can add some more buttercream using a piping bag at any point.

20 Continue smoothing out the buttercream until clean stripes of buttercream have formed and you're happy with the overall smoothness of the buttercream.

21 Decide whether to clean the top corners with your palette knife now, or place in the refrigerator or freezer for it to harden before cutting the corners off with a small, sharp (paring) knife (see page 114).

22 To add sprinkles around the bottom of the cake, take a teaspoon and place the sprinkles around the base. Then, using the back of the palette knife, lift up the sprinkles and press them onto the side of the cake so they stick to the buttercream.

23 Take all the remaining coloured buttercream and fill up another piping bag fitted with a small star piping nozzle/tip.

Place the piping bag in a tall glass and pipe each colour down the sides of the bag so when you close it, all the colours will be inside and will come out of the end together.

24 Use the piping bag of mixed coloured buttercream to create some piped details around the top of the cake, before adding your chosen decorations.

25 Decorate the top with (your choice of) rainbow meringue kisses, coloured macarons and chocolate ruffles (see pages 138, 162 and 149).

26 Finish off with a small addition of sprinkles to mirror the base of the cake... and, of course, some edible glitter!

See page 212 for information on storing a decorated cake.

Candy land sprinkles cake

This design is definitely one of the fun ones and I would say that it is suited to a more informal event. Kids (and adults too, for that matter) get excited by the sight of an abundance of sprinkles, colours and their favourite sweets and chocolates! This cake is not only fun to make, but serving and eating the cake is just as enjoyable. This is quite different to the other buttercream applications that I have covered in this book; however, it still requires some specific techniques.

Swiss meringue buttercream quantities for a candy land sprinkles cake:

15CM/6IN CAKE
150g/5½oz egg whites;
300g/10½oz/1½ cups caster sugar;
300g/10½oz/1⅓ cups unsalted butter

20CM/8IN CAKE
200g/7oz egg whites;
400g/14oz/2 cups caster sugar;
400g/14oz/1¾ cups unsalted butter

25CM/10IN CAKE
250g/9oz egg whites; 500g/1lb 2oz/
2½ cups caster sugar; 500g/1lb 2oz/
scant 2¼ cups unsalted butter

1 Crumb coat your cake and put it in the refrigerator or freezer until the buttercream has set really hard – you want it to get as firm as possible.

2 Line a baking tray with baking paper, then pour over 150–200g/5½–7oz of hundreds and thousands sprinkles and shake the tray until they spread out into a thin, even layer.

Photo Steps Continue Overleaf _____

I try to find the most pastel-coloured sprinkles that have also been coloured naturally, as they are more pleasant to eat!

3 When the cake is very cold, place it back onto the turntable.

4 Similar to the Naked Cake (see page 174), spread out a thin layer of buttercream over the cake but only over the sides, avoiding the top for now.

5 Smooth this buttercream out with the side scraper until the layer is as even as possible.

6 Clean off any excess buttercream that has come upwards around the corners of the cake and leave some buttercream on the palette knife to one side.

7 Place a new 15cm/6in cake board on top of the cake and use your palette knife to detach the cake from the board it's already on (on the turntable).

Slide your palette knife right under the cake and it should lift off easily!

8 Hold the cake from underneath and carefully place it sideways on top of the tray with sprinkles.

This is why the cake has to be as cold as possible!

9 Roll the cake over the sprinkles until the outside of the cake is fully coated.

If you need to redistribute the sprinkles, lift up the cake and shake the tray to spread out the sprinkles again.

10 If any areas aren't covered with sprinkles, you can use your hand to press some against the cake and they should stick to the buttercream.

11 Spread the reserved buttercream on your palette knife onto the original/first cake board in preparation to re-adhere the cake to it.

12 Carefully lift the cake from the sprinkles and place it back onto the cake board on the turntable and press down to secure it in place.

Some sprinkles may fall off at this point so just be aware!

13 Clean your palette knife from buttercream and use the back of the palette knife to press the sprinkles against the cake to ensure they are stuck onto the surface, especially around the bottom edge.

14 Swipe across the top corners of the cake to clean any excess of sprinkles at the top and place the cake back in the refrigerator for 10–15 minutes to allow the sprinkles to set. Meanwhile, prepare some dark chocolate ganache (see page 62) for dripping.

15 Apply the dark chocolate drips to the top of the cake (see pages 122 or 124), then wait until the drips have set before decorating.

Bear in mind that whether you're applying the chocolate drips using a palette knife or piping bag, the drips won't fall as easily over the sprinkles as they would do over buttercream because the surface isn't as smooth.

16 Now it's time to go crazy with the decorations! I love using colourful meringue lollipops (see page 140) to decorate a candy land cake. I choose three lollipops and place them into the top of the cake at different heights. I then place a selection of favourite sweets and chocolates on top of the cake, cutting some in half to expose their cross section and using multicoloured sweets to enhance the colourful nature of the cake. Sometimes I also place a few to one side at the bottom of the cake. I finish a candy land sprinkles cake with a dusting of edible glitter for that extra wow factor!

See page 212 for information on storing a decorated cake.

STACKING A CAKE

A stacked or tiered cake is every cake maker's dream. The taller the cake, the more room to decorate and the bigger the overall impact the cake has. The possibilities are endless.

A stacked cake is also every cake maker's nightmare. From the fear of it toppling over to it getting ruined in transit, it's hard to fully relax until a tiered cake is safely set up at a venue looking just as good as it did when it left your kitchen.

In order to avoid this nightmare, a tiered cake has to be built up properly inside. No cake, however strong the sponge or buttercream is, can withstand the weight of a cake on top without extra support. In this chapter, I will guide you through exactly how to prepare a three-tier cake for stacking and how to put it all together without the stress! If you are making a taller cake with more tiers, the process is exactly the same.

Preparation and tools

Without sounding too obvious, a tiered cake is a lot taller than a regular cake, which means it has to be much more stable. Before you begin stacking, make sure that you have enough room in your refrigerator to store the cake. I much prefer stacking a cake in my kitchen and travelling with it as a whole cake rather than taking the cake tiers separately and stacking them at a venue. The main reason for this is because buttercream softens during transit and while it's possible, it's much harder to fix up at a venue! However, I am also aware that not everyone has a refrigerator or car that's tall enough for a sizeable tiered cake, so, of course, work with what you have and if you need to travel with a separated cake, then try and find a refrigerator or freezer on the other side to assist you!

It's easiest to stack a cake when the tiers are extremely cold. When I know I have a stacked cake to make, I give myself an extra day to ensure that the cake has the maximum refrigeration time. Remember, once the cake has buttercream on the outside, the sponge inside is airtight and will stay fresh, so don't be afraid of keeping cakes refrigerated. I make sure I have enough room in my refrigerator for the stacked cake, which usually means that a shelf has to come out and some rearranging takes place, too. Once you have your refrigerator ready, it's time to prepare everything else.

You will need

STRONG CAKE BOARD
either a cake drum or an MDF wooden cake board to build/assemble the cake on.

EXTRA CAKE BOARDS
the same size as each cake tier and additional cake boards
5cm/2in larger than each cake tier.

ONE LONG WOODEN DOWEL
a dowel is a long, thick wooden (or plastic) stick that will sit through
the centre of the entire cake to prevent it from moving.

**JUMBO PLASTIC STRAWS/SHORTER WOODEN DOWELS/
BAMBOO SKEWERS**
to support each cake tier from the one above.

CENTRE GUIDE
to measure where the centre of the cake board is.

ELECTRIC DRILL!
to drill a hole through the centre of some of the cake boards.

DOUBLE-SIDED STICKY TAPE
to attach the drilled cake boards to the larger boards.

EXTRA (LEFTOVER) BUTTERCREAM
to seal between the tiers of cake.

Preparing your cakes
for stacking

As already mentioned, no cake can withstand the weight of another cake without added support. Each tier of cake has to be built on its own cake board, so once it's stacked, the dowels and straws/wooden skewers are holding up the board, not the cake. The largest tier of the cake doesn't need an extra cake board underneath, it can go straight onto the cake drum. Prepare the larger tier as usual and leave it to set in the refrigerator. For the smaller tiers, complete the following process.

1 Prepare your cake boards: For each tier (except the largest/bottom tier), you will need a board the same size as the cake and a board that is 5cm/2in larger than the cake. For example, for a 15cm/6in tier, you will need a 15cm/6in cake board and a 20cm/8in cake board.

2 Take the boards that are the same size as the cakes and use a guide to mark where the centre is. If you don't own a guide, cut a circle from a piece of paper the same diameter as the board and fold it in half four times, making a cone shape. Snip off the pointed end of the cone with scissors and open the paper out again. Align the paper to the board and the small circle will show where the centre is.

3 Place each marked board on top of a tall cup and drill a hole through the middle of the board, large enough so your centre dowel fits through it.

4 Attach these drilled boards to the larger boards with some double-sided sticky tape. You should now have a double-layered cake board for each tier of cake (except the largest/bottom tier). For example, I have one for my 15cm/6in tier and one for my 10cm/4in tier, then just a single cake board for my largest/bottom 20cm/8in tier.

5 Build the cakes up as you usually would directly onto these top (drilled) boards. Begin by attaching the first layer of sponge to the smaller board with buttercream, and pipe on layers of buttercream in between the remaining sponge layers just like a regular cake.

6 Crumb coat and decorate the cake as usual. The smaller cake board of each pair should now be completely hidden under the cake.

7 Chill all the tiers in the freezer for 30 minutes or in the refrigerator for at least 1 hour until the buttercream is firm (the longer they're in the refrigerator, the easier the next stage will be).

2

3

4

6

6

6

Assembling a tiered cake

By this point, your cake tiers have been correctly prepared and are ready for stacking. There is no doubt that this can be a daunting task as you're suddenly faced with multiple tiers and a much taller cake but try and relax and enjoy the process. As long as your cakes have been built properly and everything is in place, there is no reason to stress! Again, cold cakes are key to making this process as stress-free as possible. There may be times when the tiers need to be re-aligned and moved around but that's all part of the process. After all, any fingerprints or dented buttercream can all be hidden with decorations after!

3

5

1 Take the largest tier, in this case the 20cm/8in one (this will be the bottom tier), and place it onto your turntable, then fill a piping bag with any leftover buttercream.

2 Mark the middle using the guide (or piece of paper) that you used earlier and insert the tall wooden dowel, making sure it's straight. I use a side scraper to help line it up and then look at it from all angles to make sure it's completely vertical.

Now is a good chance to make sure the wooden dowel isn't too long for the tiered cake. Compare your tiers of cake with the length of the dowel and if needed, you can trim the end of the wooden towel using scissors or pliers as we don't want the dowel coming through the top of the cake once the final tier is placed on!

3 Insert 5–6 jumbo plastic straws (or 5–6 shorter wooden dowels or wooden skewers, trimmed to the

Photo Steps Continue Overleaf _____

correct height) directly into the cake, spacing them around the central dowel about 5cm/2in from the centre, then trim the straws to the same height as the cake so they sit flush against the top.

You may need to pull each straw out a little to cut it before pushing it all the way back in.

4 Take the next (middle) cake tier from the refrigerator and insert 2–3 jumbo plastic straws (or 2–3 shorter wooden dowels or wooden skewers, trimmed to the correct height, as before) and cut them flush against the top of the cake, avoiding the very centre as that will be for the central dowel to come through.

5 Pipe a small amount of buttercream on top of the larger cake for the smaller (middle) tier to adhere to.

6 Using a palette knife, carefully remove the smaller (middle) tier from it's larger cake board so you are only holding the cake with the same size board underneath.

Make sure there is no tape left underneath the board of the smaller tier!

7 Place this (middle) tier on top of the larger (bottom) tier by lining up the hole in the cake board with the dowel. Lower the cake until the dowel comes through the top and the cake sits on top of the larger tier, then gently press the cake to secure it to the bottom tier.

Because the cake is cold, touching the top of the cake shouldn't affect it too much, but if you want to be safe, cut and use a small piece of baking paper to avoid touching the cake directly with your hands.

8 Fill in the gap between where the tiers meet with some buttercream using a piping bag.

9 Carefully use the side scraper to remove any excess buttercream from where you just piped.

10 Pipe a small amount of buttercream on top of the middle tier that was just placed on the cake.

11 Take the smallest (top) tier from the refrigerator and remove it from the larger board and place it on top of the middle cake tier, lining it up with the central dowel and the hole in the cake board.

The central dowel won't go through the top of the cake

if you've measured it properly (see step 2).

12 Repeat the process of filling in the gap between the tiers and cleaning it off with the side scraper.

You don't need to insert any jumbo straws/wooden dowels/wooden skewers into the smallest tier as it won't be supporting another tier on top.

13 Now your tiered cake is stacked, so you can decorate it however you wish!

It is best to refrigerate the whole cake to set the buttercream, but if you don't have room in your refrigerator, then the decorated cake can be served straight away as the cake tiers are still cold.

I can't stress enough how important it is to keep the cakes as cold as possible when stacking. It minimizes the risk of ruining the smooth buttercream on the outside of the cakes and makes the whole process a lot less scary, too!

Top Tips

• I leave the stacked cake in the refrigerator for about an hour or overnight before adding decorations in order for the cake to set as a whole.

• To add drips on top of a tiered cake, I either add them to each tier before stacking and let the drips set, or pipe them on after stacking. The method of applying drips with a palette knife doesn't work once the cake is stacked because there isn't enough space to move around.

• When delivering a stacked cake at a wedding, for example, I like to add on the decorations once it's at the venue. This means that I travel with a plain (buttercream-iced) stacked cake and take my decorations separately. This avoids any decorations falling off and getting damaged or destroyed during transit.

EXTRAS

By this point, you've made and perfected your beautiful cake, but that's not the end of it! Decorating a cake is only half of the work, especially if you are running or starting a cake business. People underestimate the organization, time management and logistics surrounding a cake! In this chapter, I cover a few extra tips to take into consideration after making and decorating a cake.

Storage

One of my most frequently asked questions is "What's the best way to store a cake?" Unfortunately, the answer isn't so simple because it really depends on the cake you are making. For example, as already mentioned, certain decorations have different storage requirements and shelf lives. In general, decorations should be added to the cake as last minute as possible so they can be stored individually in the best way.

A buttercream cake should be refrigerated for as long as possible before being displayed or eaten. Not only does this keep the cake fresher for longer, but it also protects the buttercream from getting dented when adding decorations at a later stage.

The cake will then need to be taken out of the refrigerator however long before being served to ensure the buttercream softens up again. Of course, the time between taking the cake from the refrigerator to serving depends on the environment, as warmer temperatures will soften the buttercream a lot quicker than cooler ones.

Even though we all pray for warmer weather during the cooler months, decorating a cake in the winter months is a dream for cake decorators! The cake is able to stay out of the refrigerator for a few hours without the buttercream getting too soft. This is also possible in the summer months if air-conditioning is readily available. Basically, butter and buttercream don't like heat! So try to avoid it to keep your cake happy!

In general, a buttercream cake is at its best if eaten within 5 days if kept in the refrigerator. Once a cake is covered in buttercream, it will not dry out in the refrigerator. The sponge is totally airtight in the buttercream so it keeps the cake fresh.

Note: If keeping a cake in the refrigerator, make sure any items with an odour that are also in there are completely sealed. Dairy absorbs scent, and no one wants a cake that tastes like the vegetable drawer… I learnt that from experience!

Packaging and transport

You've created this beautiful showstopper, stored it perfectly and now you face the challenge of getting it to the event venue. It may seem like the most daunting task; however, as long as you handle the cake with care and follow a few guidelines, the cake should arrive in perfect condition.

Firstly, it's important to package the cake safely. Depending on where you are based, various cake boxes are available. Whether it's extra tall, a reusable box or one that you've put together yourself, if the cake fits inside the box with enough room for the decorations, too, then the cake will be safe for transport. Ideally, the cake board should fit snugly inside the box so it doesn't move during transportation. If the box is slightly larger than the cake board, I like to attach a small piece of double-sided sticky tape to the bottom (inside) of the box before I insert the cake. Cakes are usually quite heavy so won't move around too much, but it's better to be safe than sorry.

Every cake maker's nightmare is to arrive at a venue with a cake that's been bashed or fallen over, so here are my top transport tips to make the journey a little less stressful.

1 It may sound obvious, but make sure whoever is holding the cake is holding it from the bottom of the box and keeping it level at all times.

2 Place the cake box on the floor of the car, ideally in the boot or in the front passenger seat footwell rather than on someone's lap or on the seat itself. It's the safest place for the cake to be.

3 To prevent the box from sliding around, place a non-slip mat underneath the cake box (either a drawer liner or yoga mat or turn over the car floor mat so the rubber side is facing upwards).

4 When travelling with the cake, turn up the air conditioning to medium/full and have it pointing in a downwards direction towards the cake (bring a jumper with you for the journey!). If you don't have air-con, then turn the temperature dial to the coolest setting.

5 Drive slowly! Especially around corners and over bumps. Again, this is an obvious point, but it's easy to forget you have a cake in the car.

6 When you arrive at the venue, either take the cake from the car and place it straight into the refrigerator, or carefully remove it from the box and carry it to it's display area.

Top Tip

Always bring spare buttercream, a palette knife and scraper, as well as extra decorations with you just in case. In the worst-case scenario, if the cake is accidentally knocked en route, you can touch it up at the venue.

How to cut a tall cake

Funnily enough, I rarely cut a cake myself. However, I do have a couple of tricks to not only cut a cake efficiently, but to get the most slices out of the cake as possible! Seeing as these buttercream cakes are taller, smaller slices are cut, which means a small cake of 15cm/6in can actually go a long way!

Before you cut the cake, remove any decorations from the outside, especially if it's too hard to cut through (for example, fresh flowers or isomalt). If the decorations are edible, place them onto a plate and serve them separately. It's much easier to cut a plain cake!

Portion guides for finger slices

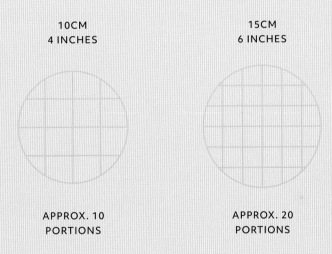

10CM
4 INCHES

APPROX. 10
PORTIONS

15CM
6 INCHES

APPROX. 20
PORTIONS

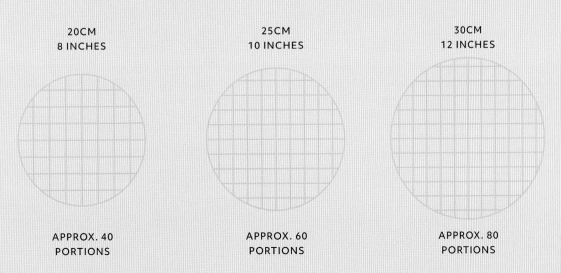

20CM
8 INCHES

APPROX. 40
PORTIONS

25CM
10 INCHES

APPROX. 60
PORTIONS

30CM
12 INCHES

APPROX. 80
PORTIONS

Finger slices

1 Using a bread knife, cut a slice straight across the whole cake about 2.5cm/1in in from the edge.

2 Let this slice gently fall onto a chopping board so it's lying flat.

3 Cut 2.5cm/1in finger slices directly from the slice lying on the chopping board.

4 Each slice will have the full four layers of cake. You also have an option to cut them in half for smaller slices.

5 Repeat the process by cutting another 2.5cm/1in slice straight across the whole cake again.

6 Place onto the chopping board and cut into smaller finger slices, then serve.

7 Continue in the same way until the whole cake is cut.

Triangle slices

1 Cut directly into the cake, making sure the tip of the knife is in the centre of the cake.

2 Move the knife about 45° and slice through the whole cake again.

3 Rather than taking out the whole slice, cut through the slice horizontally and take out the top half.

4 Then remove the bottom half (each of these half-slices should have two layers of cake) and serve.

5 Continue in the same way until the whole cake is cut.

Or

1 Cut directly into the cake, making sure the tip of the knife is in the centre of the cake.

2 Move the knife about 45° and slice through the whole cake again.

3 Take out the whole slice and rest the slice down on a chopping board.

4 Cut the slice in half (so each half-slice has two layers of cake) and serve.

5 Continue in the same way until the whole cake is cut.

In the unlikely event that there is any cake leftover, the exposed sponge will need covering before it's returned to the refrigerator. Covering all exposed areas with clingfilm, or with a thin layer of buttercream, will prevent the exposed sponge from drying out. If the cake has already been completely sliced, keep the slices in an airtight container in the refrigerator.

Cake and buttercream also freeze extremely well, so you can always freeze individual slices and take one out at a time to enjoy whenever you want! Tightly wrap individual slices in clingfilm and freeze for up to 3 months, then defrost at room temperature before eating.

#CAKESTAGRAM

Photographing my cakes has become a huge part of my job as a cake decorator. I began my cake journey at the same time that Instagram became a popular network. I photographed every cake I made and uploaded them onto the platform and that's how my profile began. It's also how I built up a portfolio of work so that customers can refer back to previous designs that I have made and request their own bespoke cake.

I still think that, to this day, a photograph of a cake doesn't have the same reaction as seeing the cake in real life (which is why I never send customers photographs before giving them the cake!). However, taking a good-quality photo of a cake is a must! After all, you've worked so hard on creating a beautiful masterpiece, you want to remember it forever!

You don't have to be the world's best photographer, but here are a few simple tips in order to capture a perfect picture.

1 HIGH-QUALITY CAMERA. Nowadays, smartphones have better cameras than some analogue or even digital cameras, so you don't need to start investing in a fancy DSLR with a hundred different lenses. However, the better the camera, the better the quality of the photo. I use a smartphone for photographing my cakes.

2 NATURAL LIGHTING. I remember the short winter days when I'm chasing the sunlight. So much so that sometimes I simply don't take a photograph of the cake because it's dark by the time I have finished it. No matter how many lights and lamps you have, in my opinion, no light is better than natural daylight. Find a place where you can set up your cake in a naturally well-lit space. Avoid direct sunlight as this can be too harsh on the cake (and may even cause it to start melting!).

3 BACKGROUND. I've always made sure that in my photographs the cake takes centre stage; therefore I use a marble or wooden surface to place the cake on with a plain/coloured background behind it. There are some undoubtedly amazing food stylists out there who use props and ingredients to set out the most intricate set-up for a stylized photo, but sometimes it can take the attention away from the cake itself.

I have always opted for a plain background so the cake pops against it. If using extra props, arrange them so the cake is still the main focus.

4 CAKE STAND. The only prop I do make use of when photographing a cake is a cake stand. Even though we decorate cakes on a turntable, displaying a cake on a cake stand makes the photograph appear polished and the cake ready for showing off!

5 REFLECTOR. A reflector is a way of reflecting the light to even out the light or lighting shining on the cake. When I take photographs at home, I set up my space with a window at one side, which means that one half of the cake is always darker than the other. Just by simply holding a reflector next to the darker side of the cake makes all the difference. If you don't have an actual reflector, you can use a chopping board or baking/oven tray covered with foil – as long as it's reflective, it works just the same!

6 EDITING. When I say editing, I don't mean editing the actual cake on Photoshop to correct any air bubbles and change the colour of the buttercream. I'm referring to enhancing the image. Most of these tools are readily built into smartphones and many online networks, too.

My go-to adjustments for editing are:

BRIGHTNESS The brighter the better! It's very easy for a photograph to be a bit dull, so I usually increase the brightness to make the image pop.

SATURATION Usually, photographs don't quite capture the real colour of the cake. I tend to increase the saturation quite a lot to make the colours of the cake stand out.

SHARPNESS As many of us are viewing these images on small screens, a sharp, crisp photograph is so important. I usually increase the sharpness on an image by 50% and it's amazing to see the difference. You can see so many details and it makes the image look much higher quality all round.

UK/US glossary

baking paper/parchment paper
bicarbonate of soda/baking soda
biscuit cutter/cookie cutter
cake tin/cake pan
caster sugar/superfine sugar
chopping board/cutting board
clingfilm/plastic wrap
cocktail stick/toothpick
demerara sugar/turbinado (or raw brown) sugar
double cream/heavy cream
food/sugar thermometer/candy thermometer
generous cup/heaping cup
hundreds and thousands sprinkles/
  colored sprinkles
icing sugar/confectioners' (or powdered) sugar
jam/jelly/preserve
jug/pitcher
kitchen paper/paper towels
loose-based/loose-bottomed
measuring jug/measuring cup
natural yogurt/plain yogurt
non-stick/nonstick
piping bag/pastry bag
piping nozzle/tip – note: both terms are included
  in all relevant entries in this book
plain flour/all-purpose flour
self-raising flour/self-rising flour
sieve/strainer
sweets/candies
vanilla pod/vanilla bean

Index

Note: page numbers in **bold** refer to illustrations.

Acknowledgements

When I sat down to write these acknowledgements, I thought long and hard about every single person throughout my life who has played a significant part. Friends and family who have helped me achieve where I am today and, in turn, enabled me to create this book. And within the mix of special people who I've met along the way, there are specific individuals to whom I owe absolutely everything.

From the very first time I baked a cake, writing a book has always been a dream of mine. That dream has now been realised due to the passionate and wonderful team at Pavilion, especially Steph, Ellen and Alice. Thank you all for believing in both my concept and vision, and for turning my baking dream into a 'hardback', beautiful reality.

To my editor, Anne. Thank you for your patience and thorough execution. Having never spoken about vanilla in such detail, it remains a unique experience – one I'm truly grateful for!

To my agent, James from Free Focus. Thank you for your continuous drive and for accepting my, let's say, 'alternative' work ethic. It was a lengthy process, but we got there in the end. I'm forever in your debt and, of course, will repay you in cake!

To the team who worked with me alongside and during the incredible book shoot. Sam, I look at you in awe – how you managed to make orange slices and piping bags so picturesque is beyond me. Thank you for your patience and for firing continuous cake-related questions – you really kept me on my toes!

To Charlie, thank you for not only supplying and designing the most beautiful props but also for your warm and uplifting energy, which was so needed during those long, intense, back-to-back shooting days.

And to Annie, I can't thank you enough for being the most efficient, like-minded and positive person as well as a truly talented food stylist. You made the whole experience of creating this book thoroughly enjoyable and stress free. Thank you for enabling me to take my vision and translating it into the most incredible imagery.

Mum and Dad. Without your patience and belief, I wouldn't have pursued the career of my dreams. Thank you for believing in me and for allowing me to take over the kitchen on a daily basis. Mum, I can't wait for the day you replace your antique scales (in lbs and ozs, of course) to electronic ones and maybe try out one of my recipes yourself?

Family, close friends and my business partner Lee'at. Your continuous support knows no bounds. You've been there throughout; you've shared my life's journey, you've been my best friends, my business advisors and number one fans, and if gratefulness were a cake, I'd make the biggest one for all of you!

To my new husband Tal, my other half, the love of my life, my best friend and my kitchen companion. Whilst layered buttercream cakes are still a new concept for you, I look forward to a sweet-filled life ahead (so long as you do the dishes).

And last but certainly not least… YOU! To every client, Instagram or YouTube 'follower' and reader, you have made this dream possible. You have been there from the very beginning of my cake journey; you have supported me all the way until today and I will always be humbled by and grateful for you all.

I hope this book is everything you wanted it to be… it certainly is for me.

Pavilion
1 London Bridge Street
London SE1 9GF

www.harpercollins.co.uk

HarperCollins*Publishers*
Macken House
39/40 Mayor Street Upper
Dublin 1
D01 C9W8
Ireland

10 9 8 7 6 5 4 3 2 1

First published in Great Britain by Pavilion
An imprint of HarperCollins*Publishers* 2023

ISBN 978-0-00-856376-9

This book is produced from independently certified FSC™
paper to ensure responsible forest management.

For more information visit:
www.harpercollins.co.uk/green

Publishing Director: Stephanie Milner
Editor: Ellen Sandford O'Neill
Design manager: Alice Kennedy-Owen
Design assistant: Lily Wilson
Designer: Kei Ishimaru
Copy editor: Anne Sheasby
Proofreader: Sarah Epton
Indexer: Lisa Footitt
Photographer: Sam A Harris
Photography assistant: Becca Jones
Food styling: Annie Rigg
Food styling assistant: Hattie Baker
Prop styling: Charlie Phillips
Production controller: Grace O'Byrne

Printed and bound in China by RRD
Repro by Rival

WHEN USING KITCHEN APPLIANCES PLEASE ALWAYS
FOLLOW THE MANUFACTURER'S INSTRUCTIONS